My Short Century

Also by Lorna Arnold

Britain and the H Bomb
(with Katherine Pyne)

Windscale 1957

Britain, Australia and the Bomb
 (with Mark Smith)
 previously published as *A Very Special Relationship*

Independence and Deterrence:
 Britain and Atomic Energy 1945-1952
(with Margaret Gowing)

My Short Century

Lorna Arnold

Published by Cumnor Hill Books

First published 2012 by Cumnor Hill Books

Inquiries should be addressed to:
  Cumnor Hill Books
  440 Cesano Ct, Apt 301
  Palo Alto, CA 94306 USA
  Email: geoff@cumnorhillbooks.com
  Web: www.cumnorhillbooks.com

Library of Congress Cataloging-in-Publication Data
Arnold, Lorna.
My short century / Lorna Arnold.
p. cm.
Includes bibliographical references and index.
ISBN 978-0-9837029-0-0
1 Arnold, Lorna. 2. Women historians of science--England--Biography
DA3.P69
940.1092

CONTENTS

Foreword

Lorna Arnold watched her father's military airship pass overhead towards the North Sea, during the First World War. She was the first girl in her village to win a scholarship to secondary school and the first in that school to win a scholarship to university. She was a friend of F.R. Leavis in the 1930s. She helped plan the post-war occupation of Germany and after VE day went to devastated Berlin to help run it. She rubbed shoulders with the spy Donald Maclean at the British Embassy in Washington, had a desk of her own inside the Pentagon and witnessed the birth of NATO. Then back in postwar London she endured years of struggle as a single mother. Only after all that, in 1959, did she begin the career that led to what might be called her life's work, as official historian of Britain's nuclear project and the author of landmark books.

This latest work by a tireless and brilliant personality now well into her tenth decade is a vivid chronicle of an eventful life, but like all good autobiographies it is more than that. By tracing a single line through so many events it not only connects us with the past but also connects the past together in refreshing ways. And better still, in a manner that is sometimes shocking, it reveals to us a part of the past as it was experienced by a woman who was almost always the only woman witnessing it. From London to Berlin to Washington and back to London again she lived in a world of men, and here she bears witness in a way they never would or could.

Lorna Arnold was plainly so full of talent that once she discovered herself as a planner and organiser in the public service no official barrier could stop her. And yet – this is the shocking part – she was stopped, by a combination of post-war changes, motherhood and abandonment. For a time she had to support herself and her children by working on the production line in a biscuit factory. Modestly, she ascribes her recovery to luck, but readers of this book are unlikely to agree. It was her abundant, undeniable ability that assured her the second career to which she has brought such distinction.

The luck, I think, has all been on the side of the world of nuclear history. Besides her relatively unsung role in the preparation of Margaret Gowing's monumental study of nuclear Britain in 1945-1952, Lorna Arnold has given us three vital works in her own right: histories of British nuclear testing in Australia, of the Windscale disaster and of the British H-bomb project. Her writing in this field is distinguished by a clear and rigorous exposition of the science, but also by a strong sympathy for the people – again, almost all of them men. That sympathy, even affection, illuminates and warms the later pages of this book. Yet there is a sentence here that is likely to surprise many. 'I am very much opposed to nuclear weapons,' she writes. Lorna Arnold is the best kind of official historian, the sceptical kind. There is no hint of partisanship or propaganda in her work and she never ducks a hard question, however much she may personally admire her characters. With subject matter so fateful and so controversial, her rigour and fairness are especially precious.

When I first met her, more than twenty years ago, she was engaged in a small and characteristic act of subversion. I wanted to write a new history of the making of Britain's first atomic bomb and I asked the Ministry of Defence to authorise the project veterans, all by then retired, to speak to me. She sat in on the meeting, a twinkle in her eye, cleverly nudging the senior official towards the consent he eventually gave. Though this was territory she herself had covered in the past, she wanted other writers to visit it too, and she made the effort to ensure the veil of secrecy was lifted a little. It was for me the beginning of a very happy friendship, and I could not begin to count how much I have benefited and continue to benefit from her support and wisdom, and from her astonishing international network of connections.

If ever it was true that a person was old in years and young in spirit, it is true of Lorna Arnold. She may be a historian, but she lives in the present and is never blasé or world-weary about today's difficulties. It has never been easy getting her to talk about her past, her astonishing closeness to some great moments in history and her personal experiences of important social change. Even to those who know her well, this book holds many surprises. It is a remarkable life and we are fortunate that she has brought her shrewdness and her storytelling gifts to bear upon it.

Brian Cathcart
London, March 2012

Introduction

This book is quite literally, a memoir, it is drawn entirely from memory. I have never been in the habit of keeping a diary or preserving correspondence. I have a small but disorganised collection of photographs but even if I had been a better record keeper, it would be of little use to me, now that I am unable to see.

There are many people in this book, and could have been many more, but the reader will find little about close family ties or intimate relationships. They belong to other people as well as me, and I would not wish to invade their privacy. Nor will the reader find much of my deepest feelings and beliefs. This is not the story of a soul; rather, it is an account of one woman's impressions of a changing world, and a record of a very long working life in some, perhaps unusual, circumstances.

The twentieth century began, we are told by historian E.J. Hobsbawm[1], in August 1914 with the outbreak of World War I and ended in 1991 with the collapse of the Soviet Union. He calls it 'The Short Century', but this short century was the most violent and destructive in history. Those seventy-seven years encompassed the horrors of two World Wars, the introduction of weapons of unimaginable power, the threat of mutually assured destruction, and forty years of Cold War, between implacable and nuclear-armed Super Powers, which threatened the very survival of human life on earth.

Yet the Short Century was not all blackness: goodness and happiness light up even the darkest of dark ages. It was also a century of unimaginable changes. No one in 1914, however prophetic, could possibly have predicted such a future and the turmoil it would bring. This was *my* Short Century; I missed the first few months of it but lived

---

[1] In his book *The Age of Extremes: A History of the World, 1914-1991*

through seventy-four of its seventy-five years, and survived it by over twenty more.

I am all too aware, from my work as an historian, of the fallibility of memory. Most recollections are memories of memories; the more often they are retrieved, the more likely they are to change. There may be errors and inaccuracies in this account, and I can do very little to check my facts. I can only promise that, to the best of my knowledge, there is no conscious fabrication or falsification. I have tried to tell the truth, if not the whole truth, as I remember it.

This project has taken many years, and has been dogged by interruptions, dead-ends, and restarts. I frequently despaired of ever finishing it, but the support of many people has helped me to complete this work.

The fact that I am still around to keep working on the book is due to the love and care of my family, especially my son Stephen Arnold, my sister Ruth Smith, and my niece Jenny Rivett. My friend Ag MacKeith served as my energetic amanuensis and editor, helping me to draft and revise. My nephew Malcolm Smith expertly recorded drafts for me and helped with revision. My friend Kate Stout organized the material, researched the pictures and fashioned the whole into a book. And my son Geoffrey Arnold was there from start to finish, from note-taking over ten years ago to handling the publication.

Throughout I was always re-energized by the encouragement and support of many friends and colleagues. I would particularly like to thank, first of all Jenny Radford for the original idea, and then Andrew Brown, Brian Cathcart, Georgina Ferry, David Holloway, Rosie Houldsworth, Madeleine Riley, John Sanderson and Hannah Sanderson.

Child's Play

Chapter 1

An Only Child

On December 7, 1915, in a quiet house in northwest London, I was wrapped in a towel and put to bed in the bottom drawer of a big mahogany tallboy. No cot and no baby clothes were ready for me, because Polly Dawson, the sister-in-law with whom my young mother Lorna was staying, was adamant that my birth was not due until January. My mother, as was common in those days, had little understanding of the 'facts of life', and had no idea when or how her baby would emerge.

My father, Ken Rainbow, was in Flanders with the Royal Naval Armoured Car Division, where the army was desperately trying to withstand the German advance. Ken was born in 1888, and his father, William Charles Rainbow, a professional landscape artist, had died young, leaving his widow, Annie Elizabeth, to bring up three small children in straitened financial circumstances.

William Charles's family helped his widow by paying for the education of the children until they were fifteen. Ken and his elder brother went to the Tiffin Boys' Grammar School in Kingston upon Thames, and their sister Phyllis went to a small private girls' school. After that, there was no contact between the prosperous Rainbow family, living in Richmond, and the little family in Kingston, where Annie Elizabeth ran a small Post Office and corner shop.

Ken and his brother both inherited their father's artistic talent. Ken left school and obtained a position at the London Ecclesiastical Insurance office, where he passed his professional exams with prize-winning success. Horace, his elder brother, worked as an architectural draughtsman. My grandmother told me that when all the main architectural firms, including Horace's own, submitted entries in the competition to design the building for the newly established London County Council. Horace boldly entered a separate design of his own. Granny said that Horace's design was the runner-up in the national competition. Sadly, Horace died tragically in his early twenties.

My mother Lorna Pearl Dawson was the daughter of teachers. Her father, Charles Dawson, had been a clever boy from a poor family in Morpeth, Northumberland, who had succeeded in gaining a London University degree by correspondence. He became a successful teacher, eventually becoming headmaster of one of the new Board schools in London, providing for the first time free elementary education for all children from five to thirteen, which had been established by the Education Act of 1870. His second wife, my grandmother, Ellen, was also a teacher. They ensured that their little daughter Lorna was well educated at one of the new Girls' Public Day School Trust (GPDST) schools, where she was a prize-winning pupil. Ellen had ambitions, unusual at the time, for Lorna to go to university and study medicine. Unfortunately, both of my mother's parents died while she was a schoolgirl, and these hopes went unfulfilled.

When Lorna left school, she applied for a Civil Service position. This involved a competitive examination, and in addition, a woman candidate had to be at least five feet tall. The petite Lorna put thick insoles in her shoes, stood very straight, and so just qualified to start work at the Head Office of the Post Office Savings Bank in West Kensington.

Lorna had three half-brothers and a half-sister, all considerably older than herself. One brother, Aubrey, worked in a senior position at the London Ecclesiastical Insurance, and became a mentor and friend to young Ken Rainbow. Aubrey provided a happy home for his sisters, Lorna and Muriel. Ken was a frequent guest, and to Aubrey's surprise, Ken and Lorna in due course fell in love and became engaged.

Shortly after the Great War began, Ken, who was a keen member of the Royal Naval Volunteer Reserve (RNVR), was called up. He and Lorna were married in March 1915 – it was an austere wartime wedding, but with a guard of honour from his fellow Reservists. They had no home, and parted almost immediately, as Ken's division was sent overseas to support the hard-pressed army in Flanders. As was the custom at the time, on her marriage Mother had to resign from her civil

My mother, Lorna Pearl Dawson

service post. She went to live with her older half-brother, Pearl, and his charmless wife, Polly.

Back from Flanders, Father was transferred to the newly created Royal Naval Air Service (RNAS). He was soon posted to an air station at Howden in East Yorkshire, from which a fleet of airships constantly patrolled the North Sea, looking for enemy shipping. Mother moved to Yorkshire to be near the air station, and we were there for nearly four years. She and I lived alone in a primitive stone cottage in a small and isolated terrace of houses called Little Kelk. Father lived at the air station and visited Little Kelk when he could.

I have an almost photographic memory of the cottage at Little Kelk. The front door opened directly from the country lane, which had no pavements or paths. There were two tiny downstairs rooms: the front door opened into the living room, and an interior door led into the adjacent brick-floored kitchen, which contained nothing but an old wooden cupboard, a table, two kitchen chairs and a large sink of rough brown stone, with no water supply and no drain. The back door opened onto a brick path, which ran along the backs of all the cottages, of which there were about six. It led to a communal wooden pump and a little shed which was the communal earth closet. Indoors, at the top of a narrow staircase that had no landing, there were two small bedrooms, quite bare, with hooks on the wall but no clothes cupboards. That was all. It was lonely, it was primitive, and it was home.

In the front room on the ground floor was a coal range that occupied one entire wall. It was of black iron, highly polished, with shining brass hinges and doorknobs, and contained a small fire grate where a coal fire was kept burning. On one side was an oven with a heavy door. On top was the hob, on which kettles and pans could be boiled. The section above the fire could be lifted out so that flatirons could be heated in the fire or pots suspended on a hook over the flames. The fire had many uses: warming the little cottage, baking, toasting bread, cooking food, or heating water on the hob. It was also used for airing laundry and drying wet clothes. For safety, a big metal fender was placed in front of it. It was a wonderful and useful creation.

Mother had grown up in London with five siblings. She was used to the company of her close family, and of her friends in the office where she worked. This pretty, young, well-educated woman, with her London clothes, London ways, and strange southern accent was no doubt something of a mystery to the other cottagers. It must have been a lonely life for her. She talked to me constantly, played with me, and took me out in my pram, or for little walks. For me, she was my whole unfolding world, and these early memories are intensely vivid and of a dreamlike happiness. Sometimes when we were out together Mother would point upwards and tell me 'Look! There's Daddy's ship!' and there, high in the sky, I would see the silver body of an airship on patrol.

One of my early memories is visiting the Howden Air Station, where I was terrified by the station's pet raven, a large, black, squawking bird. I fell over crying, and was picked up and comforted by kind naval hands. Another vivid early memory is an excursion with Father on his motorbike and sidecar. He took Mother and me to Barmston, a small, lonely bay. We sat on the sand in the sunshine and Father went into the sea for a swim. When he came out, we saw him

My father, Ken Rainbow

near the water's edge, rolling on the sand in pain. He had swum into a mass of stinging jellyfish. I was frightened, because it was the moment I first realised that grown-ups were not all powerful, and were, in fact, vulnerable. Of course, I did not know such words, but the feeling was real and shocking. I was soon reassured: Daddy was quickly better and everything was all right.

Occasionally Mother would go to the local chapel to be neighbourly, and she took me with her. I remember hearing the people sing a hymn *King's Cross to Glory and Nothing to Pay*, and someone read a Bible story which was all about the wicked Midianites, killing the 'children of Israel'. I was shocked and frightened that they should kill children. For some time thereafter I was terrified of going alone into the kitchen, in case it was full of Midianites lying in wait. Another chapel memory was of a Christmas event. Joseph, a little boy in a white nightdress, knelt gazing at the doll in a wooden box full of hay. A small girl in blue headscarf entered, and Joseph called out to her in a voice of wonder, 'Ee, Mary, lass, look what's come!' This was the first, shortest, and most memorable nativity play I ever saw.

My days were filled with songs. Mother sang all day: nursery rhymes, folk songs, happy Schubert songs, songs from *The Mikado*, music hall songs and wartime classics like *It's a Long Way to Tipperary*, *Mademoiselle from Armentières* and *Goodbye-ee, don't sigh-ee, wipe the tear, baby dear, from your eye-ee*. From babyhood my head was full of tunes, long before I could understand the words.

Sometimes we would go on outings to York. I remember seeing many men in uniform, some of whom had bandages or were on crutches. Some of the injured men were accompanied by hospital nurses, in crisp, white aprons with the distinctive red cross on the bib. I quickly decided that one day I would be a nurse like them.

One day, a ragged little boy from another village wandered into Little Kelk. When he came to our door, Mother brought him in and gave him something to eat and drink. He played with my toys and I gave him some, since he obviously had none of his own. A few days later we discovered that he had brought diphtheria from the other village, and I became very ill. Imagine an anxious mother in a remote cottage, with a sick child whom she cannot leave, no transport, no telephone, no doctor for miles, and certainly no NHS. Luckily, there was an unexpected visit from Father on his motorbike. He went off in search of a doctor, found one who had some antitoxin left, and brought him home. I do not know how long I was ill, but I remember when I recovered telling the doctor that 'Mother kissed me better.'

When he was demobilised, Father did not return to the London Ecclesiastical Insurance office where he had been employed before the War. Despite his early success there, his old post had been filled in his absence. Neither the government nor business did much at that period to safeguard the interests of men returning to civilian life after serving their country in wartime.

Wartime food shortages had alerted the Government to the dire state of agriculture, which had been severely depressed since the 1870s, and a national scheme was set up to train ex-officers as farmers. Father heard of the scheme, and was attracted by it. Farming appealed to the idealist and romantic in him, as well as being a practical solution to the

World War I Airship (Coastal Class)

problem of what to do next. He loved the English countryside, and had fond memories of a rural childhood in Berkshire.

Father enrolled in the government training scheme and went as a farm student to the great Yorkshire estate of Sledmere, not far from Little Kelk. There he was given a very thorough grounding in all aspects of agriculture, and Mother and I continued living at Little Kelk. It was a happy time. The war was over, the future seemed bright, and Mother and Father must have looked forward joyfully to their first home and a new life together.

Once Father had to take a load of grain from Sledmere to the mill for grinding, and Little Kelk was on his way. So he stopped for a mug of tea and an apple for Tom, the big black cart horse, and then, for a treat, he lifted me on to the top of the grain sacks in the wagon for a ride. We drove along the quiet lanes, where the hedges were full of big white convolvulus flowers, and Father stopped to pick long ropes of them for me. I wanted to explore the windmill, but when we arrived, I could not go in because the miller's children had measles. Contagious disease was a constant feature of childhood in those days; it was common for communicable diseases, such as measles, mumps, whooping cough, and chicken pox to run through families.

Towards the end of Father's training, Mother and I moved to Kingston upon Thames. Father was going to complete his training, and then find a farm to rent. Meanwhile Mother was expecting another baby, so we went to stay with Father's mother, Annie Elizabeth, my Granny. This was a bewildering change for me. After the quiet of Little Kelk, Kingston seemed very large and noisy, with the crowds, the clangour of the trams, and the sound of boots and bagpipes as Scottish soldiers from the nearby barracks marched down the street. The ground floor of Granny's house was a small corner shop and Post Office, which she ran. The shop bell tinkled all day and there was endless coming and going.

Since the house was on the corner, the room I slept in had windows that looked out onto two busy roads. The trams used to come down the road and round the corner, and I could see the lights swinging and hear the wheels clanking. I liked the trams in Kingston, and enjoyed going for a tram ride. They had an open upper deck, with seats of wood, where it was pleasant to ride in good weather. In wet weather, you would unhook the waterproof apron attached to the seat in front and use it as shelter from the rain.

The house itself was full of novelties: gas light, a white enamelled kitchen sink with real taps, a gas cooker, and an indoor water closet. We had had none of these conveniences at Little Kelk. There was also a pretty garden. I usually played outside. A side street was quiet enough for me to be able to ride my wooden scooter or bowl my hoop along the pavement, but Richmond Park was only a few minutes' walk away, and there I could run about and play to my heart's content. I think with great pleasure of the simple toys of my childhood: hoops, spinning tops, Sorbo balls, skipping ropes and little wooden Dutch dolls with their stick-like limbs and their funny painted faces. I also had my beloved golliwog, homemade from old black stockings by my Auntie Phyl.

Granny, who was in her late sixties, was beautiful even as an old lady, with her slim and upright figure, her rose and ivory complexion, her large blue eyes, her pile of snowy hair. She had a beautiful singing voice – a contralto, and her sister Louisa a fine soprano, but both were quite untrained. When they were young, a music impresario heard them singing in an oratorio concert and offered to take them to London and train them for a musical career. Their father indignantly rebuffed him, without even consulting his daughters.

Other members of her family had fine voices. Uncle Arthur Wallis wrote songs and later set up a music school in Ealing with his wife. He taught singing and she taught elocution. One of Granny's stories was that Uncle Arthur wrote the song *If You Were the Only Girl in the World*

Lorna Rainbow, aged 1

and sold it for a fiver to a friend of his, a music hall composer in need of a song to meet a deadline.

Granny's voice remained very true and sweet, although it got smaller as she got older. She used to sing the whole of the Messiah through to me when I was very small, until, like her, I knew it by heart. My mother's preference was for Schubert's songs.

My father's sister, Auntie Phyl, also lived with Granny. As a young girl, she had been educated at a private girls' school, thanks to the assistance of the wealthier branch of the Rainbow family. It was at school that she encountered the class consciousness that was so prevalent at the time. She had a good school friend, Marjorie Daunt, whose father was an Army officer. Marjorie later told Phyl that the headmistress had called Marjorie and her sister Olive in one day and said 'Now you must not play with Phyllis Rainbow. It is not suitable. You are the daughters of an Army officer, and her mother is in trade. She's a nice little girl, I have nothing against her, but it is not suitable for you to play with her.' The Daunt sisters did not play with Phyl at school, but ignored the advice at home, and the three girls became lifelong friends.

Like her brothers, Phyl's school funding came to an end when she was fifteen. She took a secretarial course, where she learned typing and shorthand, and secured work as a typist. For most of her adult life, she was employed by the Gas Light and Coke Company in Westminster, eventually becoming secretary to the Chairman.

Phyl was in her late twenties when Mother and I moved in with her and Granny. She was one of the many women who did not marry after World War I, when so many men were lost. She had a passion for children, and I was the first child in the family, as well as the daughter of her beloved brother. She treated me with great affection, giving me presents, making me dresses and toys, and thoroughly spoiling me.

While Mother and I were staying in Kingston, Granny took me to visit an old lady called Great Aunt Lou. I was dressed in my best brown velvet frock and my button-up boots, and after my hair had been particularly well brushed, Granny and I went off to Kew. In a road near Kew Gardens, with a view of the Pagoda, we came to a big, dark front door, and were admitted by a maid who took us to the Mistress's Room. The house was gloomy, with sombre wallpaper, massive furniture, dark window curtains and plush table covers. It was not a cheerful place.

Great Aunt Lou, a stout old lady in a tight black dress, did not seem very pleased to see us, and greeted us without smiling. We were not asked to stay for tea, and left quite soon. I was glad to be out-of-doors, and to get back to Kingston and my lovely Mother.

It was not until years later that I understood the reason for this joyless visit. Great Aunt Lou Rainbow was the eldest sister of Granny's long dead husband, William Charles Rainbow, the artist. I suppose that Granny hoped that after so many years, she could renew the family connection by presenting me to the head of the family as William Charles's grandchild. Her strategy was clearly a failure; I did not delight the eyes or warm the heart of Great Aunt Lou, who was quite unmoved by my good manners, my brown velvet dress, or my auburn hair that was so like her brother's. Neither Granny nor I ever saw or heard from her again.

Granny (Annie Elizabeth Rainbow) and Lorna,
in her brown velvet dress - circa 1921

In July of 1921 my little sister Hilary was born in a Kingston nursing home. I was thrilled and delighted. Since I had prayed insistently for a little sister, this convinced me of the efficacy of prayer. I was disappointed later in life to find that prayer was not always so reliable. I was no longer an only child, though it was some years before my new sister became conversable; my usual companions were still adults. As a family of four, we moved into our new home, Flexford Farm near Guildford, in the autumn of 1921.

Chapter 2

Farm Life and School Days

In the autumn of 1921, my family and I arrived at our new home, the white farmhouse of Flexford Farm. It was situated on the north side of the Hog's Back, a great chalk ridge that runs from Guildford to Farnham, at the western end of the North Downs. The north side of the ridge is somewhat bleak but very beautiful. The farmhouse seemed enormous to a five-year-old, especially after the tiny cottage at Little Kelk. The garden, too, seemed vast, and there were no other houses nearby. Father carried Mother through the wide green front door and over the threshold into our first home.

We explored the ground floor. A hall led to a back door to the kitchen garden, and to the right there was a long living room with two fireplaces and a window at each end. On the other side of the hall were a small, rather dark sitting room and the kitchen. A wide staircase in the hall went up to a landing, with four bedrooms and a box room. I was unaware of the lack of piped water, or gas and electricity, or a bathroom and lavatory. There was not even a kitchen range such as the Little Kelk cottage provided.

In the kitchen were a deep stone sink and an enamel bath with a wooden cover. In one corner was a large brick structure, taller than me, which was mysteriously called 'the copper'. I thought a copper was a brown coin – a farthing, ha'penny or a penny – but I later learned a lot about the purpose of this kitchen copper.

I discovered the linhay, a wooden lean-to built against the exterior wall of the kitchen, almost hidden beneath white flowering clematis. It contained a coal bunker, an earth privy, a tool bench, and an enormous mangle with a heavy iron frame and powerful wooden rollers, especially dangerous for small fingers.

Another mysterious area was behind a locked door in the hall. Brick stairs led down into a dark, cold cellar with stone shelves and a strong smell of damp and mould. I discovered that our home was only part of a bigger house, the rest of which was locked and empty. Whoever built this spacious and externally handsome house, in its fine hillside situation, must have had considerable pretensions, but these were belied by the lack of facilities.

Behind the house and kitchen garden was an orchard with old fruit trees: apple, damson and cherry. The biggest of all was a gnarled and aged pear tree, grown to the height of a forest tree. It was wonderful for climbing and produced vast quantities of small pears. In the lush grass under the trees grew many wild flowers: primroses, violets, delicate wood anemone, and also the poisonous lords-and-ladies.

Not long after our arrival, Granny and Auntie Phyl gave up their shop and home in Kingston upon Thames and came to live with us. Auntie Phyl continued to travel up to her office in London every day. It was a long journey. First there was a mile walk up the hill to the nearest bus stop, then about three miles in the bus to Guildford, and then a train journey to London, which took about forty minutes, followed by a walk over Westminster Bridge from Waterloo to her office. She had to leave very early every morning to get to work in Westminster.

Flexford Farm was to be our family's home for ten years. My sister Hilary was followed, in quick succession, by two more sisters, Rosemary and Ruth, and then just before we left Flexford Farm our brother Geoffrey was born. The house quickly filled up and no longer seemed roomy.

The farm buildings – the barn, cowshed, stable and cart shed – were almost out of sight at the bottom of the hill. The barn, large, dark and sweet smelling, was a splendid hiding place and play area. The stable was home to our two carthorses, which my father sometimes helped me to ride, though straddling their broad backs was nearly impossible for my short legs. The horses were sleek and powerful; they were initially intimidating, but I quickly learned that they were gentle and friendly, accepting apples in their velvety soft mouths. In the poultry yard and hen houses there were comfortable-looking hens with their beautiful feathers, some white, some russet red, running free in the open, pecking for food.

The cowshed was a delightful place too, especially at milking time when the cowman sat down on his three-legged stool, rested his head on the cow's flank and began to squirt milk rhythmically into the milk pail gripped between his knees.

It was a mixed farm. Father grew crops and raised dairy cows. The arable fields, high on the steep, chalky hillside, made for killingly hard work for men and horses. The lower-lying meadows were gentle and beautiful, especially the cowslip meadow, where the luxuriant grass was full of fragrant clumps of golden cowslips, and under the hedges grew violets and a variety of wild orchids. Here the cows grazed contentedly. You could tell from the taste of the milk which field they had grazed, and the taste from the cowslip meadow was heavenly.

All the cows had names, and we knew them all like friends. In time, I observed that some familiar faces had disappeared from the herd. I was told that this was because they were getting old and did not give much milk, so they had been sold. I began to wonder – if we wanted to get rid of them, why another farmer would want to buy them? I had been once to the cattle market in Guildford and did not like it. Could our cows, and the little unwanted bull calves, have been sold to a butcher? I did not ask, partly because I did not want my suspicions to be confirmed.

One Sunday dinner time I left the meat on my plate and Granny scolded me. I explained that the meat might have come from Norah, whom I had not seen for a while. In any case, it was from a cow, and cows were my friends.

'You are a silly wilful child,' Granny said. 'You will probably grow up weakly and a burden to your parents and die young.' She mentioned *pernicious anaemia*, which sounded awful. I sat at the dinner table all afternoon, weeping into my plate, but obstinate. I did not know the word 'vegetarian', or that there were such people, but I became one that day.

With a few lapses, when circumstances were overpowering, I stopped eating meat. I found quiet support from Mother. After a time I realised that the production of milk, butter and cheese were not innocent and independent activities, but were part of a vast system that included not just the meat industry but large-scale production of leather and other products, for which there were then no synthetic alternatives. I did not discuss this with anybody, for I did not know anybody who was interested, but I thought long and hard, and decided that the world was so complicated that one could only fudge. I have been a vegetarian all my life.

My romantic notions of becoming a nurse, with starched coif and apron, came to an end after we moved to Flexford Farm. The doctor recommended that I have my tonsils removed, and I was sent to a hospital in Guildford for an operation. In those days, the hospital organized tonsillectomies on production-line principles. I was put into a bed in a ward with at least ten other children who were also to have their tonsils removed that day. I was not sure what might happen, and I awaited the procedure unconcerned, fascinated by the lovely gleaming bedpan that I had been allocated, unaware of its use. Eventually, an orderly took me upstairs to the theatre. We waited on a bench near the door, and I still had no idea of what was about to happen. Then another orderly carried out a child who had just had his tonsils out; he was limp in the orderly's arms, he seemed dead, and his white gown was stained with blood. I panicked. Although I was usually a very compliant child, I screamed and kicked and fought when I was brought into the surgery, convinced that I was going to be killed, until the mask covered my face and the anaesthetic had its effect.

I woke up back in the ward with a very sore throat. The ward was full of crying children. I wanted my mother and home, and I never wanted to be in a hospital again. Thus ended my childish ambition to be a nurse.

We encountered few people outside our own family, but we did meet farm workers, and also vagrants who were a feature of the countryside and part of the seasonal workforce. They were solitary men, usually ex-servicemen, whom the end of the Great War had left rootless, homeless and unemployed, some suffering from old war injuries or shell-shock (not then recognised as Post Traumatic Stress Disorder). They seemed to have no family or close friends. They were gaunt, unwashed, unkempt, ragged, and they lived rough. I would sit on the grass talking to one who regularly camped on our farm – an unlikely friend for a little girl, but my parents apparently saw no cause for alarm. Old Jim may have looked sinister, but he was gentle and courteous to me, and I marvelled at his stories of his childhood, of his life in the army, in South Africa, the Jameson Raid, and the Great War.

He lived in a shelter near the entrance to a disused chalk pit. His simple home was made by bending hazel saplings to the ground and pegging them, then covering them with old sacks or tarpaulin. Outside the entrance, he set up a tripod of stripped boughs under which he could light a fire. Every week he went to the nearest town to buy a loaf, cheese, tea, a joint of bacon, a tin of condensed milk, tobacco and the *News of the World*. He made strong sweet tea by boiling some tea leaves in a blackened old tin can hung over the fire. His joint of bacon was boiled in the same can. His invariable diet was bread, cheese, cold bacon, strong tea, and chewing tobacco.

Miles of trudging in broken, badly fitting boots took their toll on Old Jim's feet. From time to time Mother would bring him into the kitchen and fetch a bowl of water, soap and scissors. She would then wash his filthy feet and set to work on his corns and calluses and overgrown horny toenails. Old Jim would return soon after with a grateful offering, a bottle of beer. 'I know you enjoy this, Ma'am,' he would say, and Mother, who did not, would drink to his health with well-simulated pleasure.

Jim once bought a copy of *Paradise Lost* from a second-hand bookstall in Guildford and read it slowly and laboriously by candlelight in his rough shelter. When he had finished it, he concluded that Milton, for all his book learning, had failed to justify the ways of God to man. I never knew where Jim went in the winter. Such homeless victims of war often developed pneumonia in the winter and found temporary shelter or death in a local hospital.

It was a very free life for us children. We wandered unhindered about the farm and the countryside, which was quiet and almost devoid of traffic. Our lives were not highly organised or closely supervised. We had so much time in which to read, play, daydream, or collect and identify the wild flowers and plants which grew in great variety and profusion. We could watch birds and listen to birdsong. We had little contact with other children, as there were no neighbouring farmhouses. Of course we had no television, very little 'wireless', and very few records. There were no shops or cinemas for miles, and no organized activities such as riding lessons, music lessons or ballet classes. Yet I was almost never bored. Certainly not while there was a diverse collection of books in the house, including *Kim, Uncle Remus*, Captain

Marryat's *Sea Stories*, Shakespeare, *The Heroes*, *Lorna Doone*, *A Tale of Two Cities* and *Westward Ho!*, and beautifully illustrated bound volumes of the *Strand* magazine. In these volumes I first met Sherlock Holmes, E. Nesbit's stories, and the strange tales of W.W. Jacobs.

Though we had much freedom to play, there were few domestic labour-saving devices, and there were endless chores too. We helped Mother in the house and on the farm: sweeping, beating carpets, and scrubbing brick or stone floors on hands and knees with buckets of cold water. There were endless other tasks such as filling and trimming oil lamps, cleaning candle sticks, sewing on buttons, darning socks and jerseys, and turning sheets 'sides to middle', which is now an obsolete skill. Doing the family wash was a laborious weekly task.

The mighty copper was the centrepiece of washdays. Early on Monday morning, we carried heavy buckets of water from the pump and emptied them into the copper. We kindled a small fire in the grate underneath. While the water heated up, a tablet of hard, yellow soap would be grated and the flakes thrown into the water and stirred with a big wooden 'copper-stick'. When the water was ready, we put in a load of laundry, which might be clothes, shirts, sheets and towels or occasionally blankets. All this was agitated with the copper-stick, then left for a time. In due course, we would remove the hot, wet clothes with the indispensable copper-stick to a large galvanised iron bath of clean water nearby. Then we rinsed them, while the next load of washing was lifted into the copper.

After a thorough rinsing, we took the clean wet washing into the linhay to be mangled. The mangle's heavy rollers, though excellent for sheets and towels, were hazardous to shirt buttons. After this, we carried the washing in a large willow basket to the part of the rickyard (a farmyard containing ricks of hay or straw) where several washing lines were strung between posts and trees. We pegged the laundry out to dry in the sun and wind, if the weather was good. In bad weather, the laundry would get even wetter, or might even freeze as hard as boards in the cold. Then next day we brought the laundry indoors to be folded, ready for ironing. With no synthetic fabrics and no electric irons, this was an exacting task.

Each flat iron had to be heated on an open fire until the temperature was judged to be right. One would take up the heavy, awkward black iron with a padded iron-holder to protect the hands, and test its temperature by holding it close to one's cheek or, more safely, by spitting on the hot metal. Too hot an iron resulted in scorch marks or even irreparable damage. Ironing was not an easy task for the inexperienced.

After a final process of airing on a clotheshorse and overhead racks, the clean washing could be folded and put away, or taken into immediate use. We all knew and sang that delightful song *Dashing Away with a Smoothing Iron*, but we were agreed that the girl who 'looked so neat and charming, in every high degree' as she did her washing was not a working farmer's wife or a cottage woman, but more like one of Marie Antoinette's make-believe milkmaids.

In 1922, nearly a year after our move to Flexford Farm, I started school. I was nearly seven, and could have started earlier, but the local elementary school was over a mile away, along a lonely country road, and it is not surprising that my parents thought it was too far for a five-year-old to walk by herself. Wanborough School, with a few neighbouring cottages, was located some distance away from the village of Wanborough. A grassy track from the lane led to the school entrance.

The lane, from the farm, like most country roads of the time, was of earth and flint, sometimes dusty, sometimes muddy, and deeply rutted. There was no traffic except for an occasional horse and cart; a car was never seen. On either side were wide grass verges and luxuriant hedges, and a clear little stream ran alongside it for part of the way. Beyond the hedges were fields and copses but I only passed two houses before I reached the small row of cottages next to the school.

The walk to school is full of happy memories: of a lovely profusion of wild flowers by the roadside – dog roses, May blossom, meadowsweet, Star of Bethlehem, and so many more; of the birds and birdsong; of tiny emerald green frogs in the puddles; of ripe hazel nuts and vivid spindleberries, hips and haws in the autumn. Then in winter – every winter – the magic of snow. In fine weather, I was often very slow, reading a book as I walked. In wet and stormy weather I would sing as I splashed through the puddles in my rubber boots and enjoyed the sensation of the rain driving against my face and running off my

Wanborough School circa 1930

oilskin coat and my sou'wester. The wild birds would be singing too. My special pleasure was a good thunderstorm.

My only fear on these lovely walks was an entirely imaginary one. At one bend in the road, there was a large and sinister looking oak tree, and I convinced myself that, centuries ago, a young man had been hanged there. I would run past that tree with my heart thumping.

The school was a two-storey building with a field all around and a little asphalt playground, and inside was a lobby with rows of washbasins and rows of coat pegs on the wall. The main part of the school consisted of a large room with a partition which divided it into two: the Little Ones and the Big Room. There were about fifty pupils, from five to fourteen years of age. One elderly, unqualified teacher looked after the Little Ones; the Big Room was the responsibility of the qualified teacher who taught all subjects to all the children, boys and girls, up to Standard Six or Seven at fourteen years old.

While in the room of the Little Ones my time was occupied in threading strings of glass beads, playing with a sand tray, making models with dreary grey Plasticine, reciting nursery rhymes and verses, and learning passages from the Psalms and the New Testament. I have never forgotten 'a certain man went down from Jerusalem to

Jericho…'. We also cut up old woollen garments and socks into small squares with small blunt nail scissors, though we never knew the purpose. This soon produced weals on young fingers and thumbs.

I had another encounter with a nurse around this time. The local council sent a district nurse to do a routine inspection of the children for common problems such as head lice and impetigo. We children stripped down to our undergarments, and presented ourselves for inspection. Still traumatised by my tonsillectomy, I attempted to run away, clad only my underwear. Clearly my infatuation with nursing was shattered.

Every morning during the winter, our teacher would put a big black kettle on the hob over an open fire. After a while she would get together fifteen or twenty enamelled mugs, put a dob of cocoa into each one, and then pour in boiling water, and stir. Sometimes there was a little sugar added, but no milk. This was given to us for our morning drink: not pleasant, and the metal mugs were uncomfortably hot.

The really important thing for the Little Ones was learning to read. We had very old, dog-eared primers from which we learnt that 'Fan had a pug' and 'Fan is in the gig'. We had no idea what a pug was, or a gig, but the illustration showed that they must be a small dog and a small carriage. Why the girl in the long frilly skirt and flowered bonnet was called Fan was a mystery to us all. Having quickly mastered Fan and her strange doings, I could read, and was transferred to the Big Room.

Girls and boys of all ages between seven and fourteen sat in close-packed rows of desks, and in front of the class was the teacher's desk and chair. On the wall behind her were a blackboard and a very pink map of the world; at one end of the room was an old piano. There was not much space for some forty children, but the room was airy, and lit by large windows on two sides. One unassisted teacher was responsible for all these pupils of various ages and greatly varying abilities. No special provision was made for children at either end of the spectrum. Schoolwork was organised in 'Standards', from the Standard One of those newly promoted to the Big Room to the Standard Seven of the fourteen year-olds who were about to leave the little world of education for the adult world of work.

Most of the children came from very poor families and many of them looked poorly, ill nourished and badly clothed. The little boys usually wore long baggy shorts made by cutting off their fathers' worn out trousers at the knees and tying the shapeless garment round their skinny little waists with string or, if lucky, a webbing belt with a snake clasp. Hand-me-down boots were usually cracked or ill fitting. Skin infections such as impetigo were common, but with no National Health Service, healthcare was dreadfully inadequate, and birth defects such as a squint or cleft palate were seldom remedied. Then every year the children were routinely stricken by infectious diseases: measles, mumps, chicken pox, even diphtheria. At that time these were regarded as rites of passage, as part of the normal pattern of childhood. Occasionally a pupil would disappear for months for a stay in the TB sanatorium, which we knew was in the pinewoods on some far away hillside in Hampshire.

How did village schoolteachers manage to teach so much to so many simultaneously? There was much learning by heart, much reading aloud and much recitation; children worked in small groups together; and the older ones helped those in the younger groups. Writing, using inkwells and steel-nibbed dip pens, was taught with great care; quick-fire mental arithmetic lessons gave us practice in rapid calculation, which has proved useful to me all my life. Nature lessons encouraged us to bring in wild plant specimens to be identified and studied. The girls learnt to sew hems and seams and to make buttonholes, and both girls and boys learnt to knit dishcloths in white cotton. In the Higher Standards we had excellent lessons on what Parliament does, how laws are made, how elections work, and what local government does.

Many lessons were devoted to drawing and painting. My father, Ken, also encouraged me to draw and sketch at home. There was lots of singing; we learnt many lovely folk songs – *The Ash Grove, Blow The Wind Southerly, Early One Morning* and many others printed in small paperback booklets with the melodies given in tonic *sol-fa* notation (*doh, ray, me*). We even learnt traditional English country dances; the desks would be pushed back to give as much floor space as possible, and Mrs Evans, our teacher, would sit at the piano and instruct us in the mysteries of *Rufty Tufty* and *Gathering Peascods*.

When the weather was fine we could go out into the playground for our breaks to play ball games, skipping and hopscotch, and round games that passed from one generation to another, such as:

The wind, the wind, the wind blows high,
The rain comes scattering from the sky.
She is handsome, she is pretty,
She's the girl from the royal city.
She has sweethearts, one, two, three,
Pray tell me who they be?

During the midday dinner break the older children would escape from the playground into the woods that grew around the school on three sides, and would go exploring, picking hazel nuts when ripe, or running wild in the fields beyond. In bad weather all the pupils were confined in the Big Room for six or seven hours except for an occasional rain-soaked dash across the playground to the row of earth closets. All this time, our teacher had to keep us under control, well behaved, reasonably happy and learning; the worst that ever happened was that one might be bored for a while.

Though I had been a late starter at school, my little sister Hilary certainly was not. When she was three, she was so envious of my good fortune that she agitated to be allowed to go too, and surprisingly she was admitted at that early age. For two or three years I pushed her to school, and home again, in a rickety old pushchair – not easy on the rough, unmade hilly lane. Sometimes she would make me late by jumping out of the pushchair on the way and going off to pick flowers or paddle in the stream. She became a pet of the elderly and rather short-tempered teacher in charge of the Little Ones, who took her to sit on her knee and allowed her to do whatever she wanted.

This elementary education was all that most of the local children would ever have. For most country children at this time, school life ended at the age of fourteen, only recently raised from thirteen. There was no Eleven Plus exam, which was not introduced until 1944, but some local authority scholarships existed that allowed a few of the more able children to transfer to secondary school at the age of eleven – either the old grammar school foundations, or the new secondary schools established by the 1911 Education Act.

Rainbow family at Flexford Farm
Father holds Hilary, Granny with Lorna behind her,
and Mother holds Rosemary

The scholarship exam was the doorway to a secondary education, but from little schools like ours, it would be an exceptional decision to enter any of the pupils. Only the brightest were entered, and some parents would reject any such suggestion because they regarded it as unsuitable for their station in life. As an adult, I have heard of several girls of my generation who obtained scholarships but did not take them up, either because their parents could not afford the school uniform or because the family needed the girl's wages. I thought that if I did not pass the scholarship exam I should have to leave school at fourteen, and go into service or to work in a shop, such as Woolworth's.

I believe that no pupil from our village school had ever obtained a scholarship or even sat the exam before 1927. On the day of the exam, the big school hall in Guildford, the rows of desks, and the awesome examination procedures all terrified me, but the papers were no problem. I particularly enjoyed the novelty of the intelligence test papers, which seemed to me like a wonderful new game. I passed, as did two other girls from Wanborough School: the teacher's daughter and the daughter of an Irish shop assistant who lived in the village and worked in Guildford. My scholarship meant that I could attend

Guildford County School for Girls, starting in September of 1927. What luck! I was to have an opportunity to continue my education.

Though I was very much a country girl, I felt a strong affinity with London. All through my childhood I had visited my mother's relations there. Mother had three much older half-brothers and a half-sister, all of whom lived in various parts of northwest London. Two of them, Uncle Aubrey and Auntie Muriel Dawson, were especially kind to me. Auntie Muriel kept house for her brother Aubrey who had done well at the London Ecclesiastical Insurance, but in contrast to my mother's heavy labour on the farm, her work seemed to be to do a little dusting and some shopping and give orders to the servants.

I loved the quiet of their house, and all their household treasures. I was especially fascinated by the big, old fashioned bathroom, with its terrifying copper geyser that belched steam and spurted scalding water into a flowered porcelain bath enclosed in a mahogany box frame. The bathroom was dimly lit by a fishtail gas lamp, with no mantle and twin flames from two small nozzles. The hall was very dark and gloomy, and a few steep steps led down into the kitchen, which was even darker and gloomier. It was always full of the latest kitchen gear, brought back by Auntie Muriel from Good Housekeeping Exhibitions at Olympia Exhibition Hall and mostly left to sparkle unused in the gloom below.

Grocery shopping with Auntie Muriel was a grand experience. We would take the Tube to the Home and Colonial Store. It was palatial, with a marble floor, mahogany fixtures and gleaming tall windows. To purchase an item, my tiny aunt would go to the appropriate counter, and perch on the very high stools provided for the convenience of the patrons. A deferential shop assistant in a white coat would inquire 'What does Madam want?' and would then take great care over her exact requirements as to the thickness and fattiness of the bacon. When they had finished, he would put the bill in a canister, which whizzed along a cable to the accounts clerk in a central kiosk. She would then repeat the process at the next counter, which might offer coffee or dairy products, until all her selections were made, and ended her visit at the central kiosk, where she settled the bill.

Aunt Muriel Dawson

The next day a smart little man with a neat horse-drawn van delivered the purchases in a handsome basket. This was in startling contrast to our infrequent visits to the village store at home, with its limited selection and densely packed shelves. We raised most of our own food, and the idea of buying eggs and butter seemed quite odd to us.

In her kitchen, Auntie Muriel would cook minute and delicate meals for herself and her brother. As children, we always felt hungry when we were staying there, although we were suitably impressed by her exquisite cuisine. They were small, fastidious people, who seemed to require little nourishment, apart from Bath Oliver biscuits, sweetbreads, omelettes, and elegant salads. A friend of Uncle Aubrey's who lived nearby used to smuggle bags of sticky buns into the house for us to eat on the quiet!

My aunt and uncle took me to many of the great sights of London: Westminster Abbey, the Tower of London, St Paul's, the British Museum, the National Gallery, and quite often to the theatre. One of my early memories of theatre was of a very young John Gielgud with Gwen Ffrancon-Davies in the first production of *Richard of Bordeaux*, by Josephine Tey. I also remember the drama of Elizabeth Barrett and her elopement with Robert Browning, in *The Barretts of Wimpole Street* at the Queen's Theatre. Theatre excursions with Uncle Aubrey were usually to Shakespeare performances at the Old Vic or to Gilbert and Sullivan operas.

Surprisingly, we also visited a church hall in a very slummy area near Euston Station, where my aunt had discovered a small enterprise run by a group of West End actors who brought dramatic performances to the ragged children of the neighbourhood. This little voluntary group had apparently no official backing. They did delightful sketches based on nursery rhymes, fairy stories and folk songs, and these largely impromptu performances were staged in their spare time between professional work. Their leader was Geoffrey Wincott, an excellent actor who was then starring in the West End in a powerful play about First World War soldiers in the, trenches, called *Journey's End*. His wife Joan Luxton was also a part of the group.

I was not the only person my Uncle Aubrey introduced to the theatre. On his trips to Shakespeare plays at the Old Vic and Stratford on Avon, he often took John Neville. John was a poor North London schoolboy who sang in the choir at the church where Uncle Aubrey was churchwarden, and in time he became one of our extended family. John Neville won a scholarship to RADA at the same time as Richard Burton, and later became a matinee idol and a famous actor. He went on to be the director of the Nottingham Playhouse before emigrating to continue his career in Canada. His biographer, J.C. Trewin, later wrote that he would never have become an actor but for Aubrey Dawson, who had fired his enthusiasm for Shakespeare and the theatre.

I have many happy memories of the visits to my London relatives, and of occasional summer holidays with them. We went boating on the Upper Thames – Uncle was an excellent oarsman – and visited Scotland. When I was eleven we went on holiday to Brittany, to the beautiful seaside resort of La Baule. My two younger sisters and I went, together with Mother, who was pregnant at the time, and one of Uncle's young protégés. My uncle paid for us all. Everything about this holiday was novel and exciting, beginning with the long ferry journey from Southampton to Saint Malo. Unlike most of the other passengers, I was not sick and thoroughly enjoyed the voyage. It was an exotic experience: the miles of golden sands at La Baule's famous beach, the aromatic pinewoods, the novelty of hearing French spoken all around, the hot chocolate and croissants for breakfast. Even the breakfast crockery was excitingly different, with its heavy cups, green and gold rimmed.

Uncle Aubrey Dawson

Our family seemed to live in two worlds: the hard work of our daily farm life, and the more sophisticated life that we experienced through the generosity of our relatives. At home we had access to books and music, but had little or no contact with others with the same interests, and very little leisure. Our family was in many ways quite self-contained. I was looking forward to secondary school, and the new experiences I would have there.

Chapter 3

New School, New Farm

On my first day at the Guildford County School for Girls (GCS) I wore my school uniform for the first time with pride, though in fact it was neither attractive nor practical. Being the eldest, I was lucky because I had it new, but it had been bought too big, so I could grow into it. There was a great class divide between the girls who could afford top quality uniforms, and those of us who had the cheaper versions, though all came from the school outfitters. The uniform was complicated.

My daily outfit consisted of woollen 'combs'[1] and a 'peter pan bodice'[2], with home-made navy-blue knickers and either a blouse or woollen jumper. Over the knickers and blouse went a box-pleated gymslip and a cardigan. Ironically, the gymslip could not be worn for gym as it was too cumbersome, and had to be removed for gym lessons, for which we wore knickers and tops. It was made of navy serge, and required frequent pressing to preserve the pleats. Out of doors it bunched up uncomfortably under your coat. I used to wonder why we girls did not wear the same kind of gymslip as our gym teacher – streamlined, unpleated, and thoroughly practical. I never asked. Our shoes were black leather lace-ups. We wore long black woollen stockings, held up by suspenders. In the summer, striped cotton dresses and panama hats were in order.

The wool and cotton of my uniform tended to wear rapidly, and I became an expert darner, wielding my darning needle and darning egg to repair my clothes. I took a certain pride in my ability to repair them

---

[1] Short for combinations, a one piece undergarment that had both a vest and legs. Pronounced 'comms'.
[2] A button-through under vest made from cotton jersey reinforced with cloth tape to prevent sagging.

neatly. All my sisters followed me to GCS in due course, and all had to wear this dreaded uniform.

The journey to my new school was very different from my walk to the village school. To reach GCS I first climbed to the top of the Hog's Back. There I caught a bus, displaying my new school bus pass, and after a few miles reached the outskirts of Guildford and the imposing iron gates of my new school. For the first year I then walked a further mile to the junior school on the banks of the River Wey. This building was a former French convent, a quiet, attractive old house surrounded by trees. During my year there, the ceiling fell in on our desks, fortunately while we were outside for games. I kept my crushed pencil box as a memento for years.

Moving to the upper school in a modern building was by no means so big a change as moving from the village school, but it was the beginning of a new stage in my school life. This school would seem very old fashioned by present standards; it was small with fewer than 300 pupils, all girls, and with a staff of unmarried women teachers. In those days any female public employee who married had to resign her post. I do not remember such a case from my own school days, although there was a rumour that one teacher had a secret husband hidden at home. The teachers represented an early generation of women graduates, and seemed to us schoolgirls to hold a very special place in society. Some girls pitied them because they had no husbands or children and had to work for their living, while some, who saw the hard and restricted lives that their own mothers lived, envied rather than pitied the teachers. For a few of us, they were exciting examples of professional women: clever, independent, free, living in their own flats or houses, and enjoying holidays abroad, then usually a privilege of the wealthy. Our teachers were an engrossing topic of conversation among us.

What did we girls think would be our future? Many hoped to become good housewives and mothers, the norm of the time; a few wished for careers as nurses, secretaries or elementary school teachers, but even those few mostly saw these jobs as an interim step until they married. For myself, I certainly did not want to follow in the footsteps of my beloved mother. Farm life offered unending hard labour, financial insecurity, and a continuous string of children to care for. While I was fond of my sisters and brother, I did not long to have children, unlike most of the girls I went to school with. I had no specific career plans, but hoped to do something that was interesting, and to do it well. In this period, women were still obtaining certain legal rights that we now take for granted. When the vote for all women who were over twenty-one came in March 1928, not long after I started school at GCS, I remember my Auntie Phyl dancing into the room chanting 'I've got the vote! I've got the vote!' It is surprising that my independent aunt, and the graduate teachers I so admired, had to wait so long for the right to vote.

From an early age boys had a much clearer sense of their futures. Sons often followed in their fathers' footsteps: working class boys followed their fathers to the mill or mine, while the sons of professionals or tradesmen often joined the family business. It was common for families to plan for their sons' futures; where they would go to school, what careers they might have. The daughters' futures were often left to chance and marriage. Even daughters of well-to-do and well-educated families often had to fight for the right to a higher education and a career.

At this time, there was no such thing as careers guidance at GCS (nor, I imagine, at other schools for young women). By the time my sister Hilary was in the sixth form, in the late 1930s, career counselling was in place, but the focus was still limited by the perspective of the period. The counsellor arranged the girls in a circle, and asked each what they wanted to be.

'Nurse,' said one.

'Primary school teacher,' said another.

Hilary had other ideas. 'I want to be an actress,' she declared.

The headmistress said gently, 'Oh, no, dear! None of my girls would ever do that sort of thing. If you can't be an actress, what would you want to be?'

'A journalist,' said Hilary. After a pause, she added 'A foreign correspondent.' 'But...' said the counsellor, 'that's a man's job.'

And she moved on to the next pupil.

I was a rather shy girl, and not always happy about the attention that I received at school from my classmates. Sometimes I wished my last name was Brown, not Rainbow, a name which often caused comments. I was red-headed, which also caused comments, and I was always at the top of the class, which while satisfying, again drew attention. Nor did I know what to think of myself. Girls were encouraged to be pretty and quiet and good. My Granny would sometimes recite:

> *Be good, sweet maid, and let who will be clever;*
> *Do noble things, not dream them, all day long:*
> *And so make life, death, and that vast forever*
> *One grand, sweet song.*

- Charles Kingsley, *A Farewell*

The somewhat Victorian sweetness and subservience of this poem well expressed my Granny's attitude towards girls, which would cause Father to sometimes ironically mutter his own version:

> *Be good, sweet maid, and if you* must, *be clever!*

I once asked my Granny if I was pretty, which resulted in a long silence as she examined my person. 'You have a very nice forehead' was her solemn judgement. Unsatisfied, I later asked my mother the same question, and received an equally unsatisfying answer. 'You are a very good child, and very well behaved. Don't dwell on your appearance; that will make you vain.' She was echoing an idea commonly held, that one should not be self-absorbed.

Her answer left me wondering about my appearance and, to a modest degree, what sort of person I should be. Was my success in school a good thing, or was being clever something that should be hidden? Was I sufficiently modest and well behaved? It was not clear what ideals of girlhood (and later womanhood) I should adhere to, and those doubts lingered for me many years. Indeed, the roles of and attitudes towards women that I found confusing at that time have been continuously changing throughout the twentieth century.

The teacher who most influenced me was Miss Dawes, the English mistress, scholarly and somewhat pedantic, who spent much time and trouble on me when I reached the sixth form. She read Old English and Middle English texts with me, and we studied the philological work of Otto Jespersen. I might have expected this somewhat precocious introduction would have been a help to me at university, but it was not to be the case.

I greatly enjoyed history, taught by a lively and original Scotswoman, whose apparent lack of enthusiasm for Empire Day, which celebrated the glories of the British Empire with songs and patriotic demonstrations, led some school governors to suspect her of left-wing sympathies. A less colourful character whom I greatly liked was our Latin teacher. I was glad to continue Latin studies alongside English at University, and I retain an interest in the subject.

The most inspiring teacher was Sybil Chesterfield, the first full-time music teacher at the school. She arrived two years after I joined GCS, and had an electrifying effect upon the whole school. Her elegance and beauty were in strong contrast to our other teachers, and indeed to most women we had ever met. She was as talented as she was beautiful, with a lovely voice and great musical ability, as well as being a gifted teacher. In later years the composer Herbert Howells did his best to lure her away to London to teach at St Paul's School for Girls, but she remained loyal to GCS. She quickly established a musical tradition in the school, and although she was unable to create a school orchestra, she soon had several promising and enthusiastic choirs, who would arrive early and stay late for extra choir practices. I had two great friends, a Welsh alto called Jessie Davies, and Gladys Salter, a girl with a beautiful soprano voice. We would get together to sing madrigals and part songs in our breaks. When our music teacher discovered what was going on she said 'You shall be the School Trio, and I shall take you to London to perform on the wireless.' She took us to the next music festival to compete against adult trios, and we won first place and a special commendation from Herbert Howells, who was the adjudicator. Broadcasts from London and a recital at the Wigmore Hall followed. It was all very exciting! Singing and music were not exam subjects, so some staff regarded them as unimportant and intrusive, but they became a vital part of the school's life – and certainly of mine! I am glad to hear that the tradition she began still lives on at GCS to this day.

My lifelong passion for music, especially choral music, was mainly due to this inspiring teacher, though I first was exposed to good music at home. I have sung in trios, quartets, small choirs and very large choirs, whenever I had the opportunity, until my singing voice finally left me. I am still extremely grateful to Sybil Chesterfield.

We had an admirable science teacher, but physics and chemistry played only a small part in the school curriculum, and they never engaged me. Thus I was unaware of the extraordinarily interesting scientific discoveries then being made. I had no idea, for instance, that in 1932 two scientists in Cambridge had split the atom; this fact would be central to my later life.

My relatively easy journey to and from school each day by bus and on foot came to an end in 1931 when we moved southwards from Flexford Farm to Little Prestwick Farm, near Haslemere.

The bright new prospects for agriculture that had followed the government's post-war development programme had now faded, and British agriculture suffered severely, though less publicly, from the worldwide Depression that devastated the industrial towns. Small farmers suffered especially from market conditions. When we first moved to Flexford Farm there was a feeling of enthusiasm and hope. Father could not have worked harder, and he put a huge amount of effort and thought into his farm. He was a good farmer: he was clever, knowledgeable, and hard-working, and he did his very best, but the Depression was devastating to small farmers. The rents were quite unreasonably high, even though the farm belonged to the local authority. We heard that after we left Flexford Farm, the next tenant was never able to pay the rent. The Depression was so bad, Father would say, 'I don't know which is worse, a good harvest or a bad harvest.' In a good harvest the prices plummeted, and with a bad harvest there was little to sell. Suicides were not uncommon among farmers at this time. In our neighbourhood, one of the more substantial farmers, a man who seemed most secure, shot himself in a wood near his house; it was rumoured that he had reached the point where he had insufficient money in the bank to pay his weekly wage bill.

Not all of the farmers' economic misfortunes were due simply to the Depression. While we were at Flexford Farm, Father had two old Army horses, and he was very fond of them. They were good horses, and a horse becomes a friend of the family in a way that a tractor does not. One day, Father walked into the farmhouse kitchen with a horse collar over his shoulder, looking absolutely stricken and he said

'Captain is gone. He just dropped dead.' The horse had suffered a massive heart attack while working on the hill. It was a huge shock: we were all very upset and the children cried. It was a big economic blow to Father and a sad loss to us all.

Shortly after this, Father and Mother elected to move to Little Prestwick Farm: it was smaller, with a lower rent, and would be easier to run. My parents hoped that, as a dairy farm, it would be less vulnerable to fluctuations in market prices. Grazing cows required less farm machinery and labour than the mixed farming that they had done at Flexford Farm. The new farm in Prestwick was in a beautiful position south of the Hog's Back, where the countryside was gentler, and the climate more mild.

Our first sight of it was a huge old barn with a tiled roof, built (we were told) from timbers taken from the ships of Nelson's navy. Next to the barn was an attractive brick-built granary, with a wooden staircase at the back and space for carts underneath. Between the two, a cart track led from the lane into the square farmyard, bounded by the cowshed, the dairy, and the stable for two carthorses. Opposite the entrance was the farmhouse itself, built of flint and brick, with a little walled garden in front of it, full of rose bushes and lavender. In the middle of the garden was a rose-covered stone pigsty, long disused, which later became a favourite place for the children to play. At the side of the house, just beyond a wide cart track, were the chicken run and the rickyard.

This little farmhouse, which was later featured in an upmarket magazine because of its charming appearance and historic interest, would have been an enchanting home for a small family if it had had modern amenities. Our family consisted of nine people: Mother, Father, Granny, Auntie Phyl, and five children ranging in age from a baby to a fifteen-year-old, exceeding a reasonably capacity for the farmhouse.

The house had a small sitting room, half of which was taken up by a brick hearth, with benches built in at the sides and a large chimney hood. In most weather conditions this chimney smoked so badly that the fire was seldom lit; instead heat was provided by a small oil stove sitting on the hearth where a cradle of logs should have been. This was the family's sole living room. It was here that Granny sat by the hearth

Rainbow children at Little Prestwick Farm
By height: Lorna, Hilary, Rosemary, Ruth, Geoffrey

in her old armchair, endlessly darning the socks that were piled in the workbasket next to her chair, or reading the Hardy novels that were serialized in *Tit-Bits*. A piano and a large table filled the rest of the room.

It was at this large table that much of daily life occurred. We sat round the table for meals, for letter writing, for conversation. The younger children sometimes played underneath the table, using a shelf under it as a place for hiding their small personal treasures. It was here that we did our homework, by the light of the oil lamp, which was the only lamp in the house. Other rooms were lit by candlelight. In fact, there were very often homework, tea, and bedtime drinks going on at the same time. It was not easy to concentrate on homework.

One evening I was working assiduously on a map of Australia in my geography exercise book. I took a huge pride in my maps. As I worked, one of the younger children knocked a bedtime cup of cocoa all over my carefully drawn map. I mopped and dried it as best I could, but when I handed it in the next day at school our formidable geography mistress reprimanded me. I tried to explain, and she accused me of trying to throw the blame on my little sister. I could not make her understand, and she punished me by evening detentions until the entire book with all its maps had been copied out afresh.

Next to the sitting room was a small kitchen, which had its own water supply and a coke boiler, but no cooking facilities. Our only means of cooking was an oven heated by a primus stove and a second primus for boiling. Providing meals on this for a large family was a formidable challenge, but Mother managed to feed us all, and even to bake excellent cakes and fruit pies, and to make jam.

Unlike town children living in cramped living conditions, we had plenty of space outside the house to roam. The barn provided ample opportunity for play, and comfortable corners in the hayloft were ideal for reading or study while the light permitted. It was a very free existence for us children, who wandered widely over the countryside.

As the younger children grew up and it was no longer possible for all four girls to sleep in one double bed, Father acquired a prefabricated two-roomed hut from a catalogue, to use as extra living space. It was made from single planks with no lining or insulation at all. In time the roof leaked, and we would sleep under old raincoats when we could no longer move the beds to avoid the drips. After dark, as the eldest and the last to go to bed, I was guided on my way – across the garden, over a cart track and through the rickyard – by the lines of candlelight shining through the gaps between the planks. It was very cold in the winter, and only partly warmed by a small Aladdin portable oil stove. You could see light dancing through the decorative vents on the top of the stove, throwing pretty patterns on the ceiling.

I was glad when it was decided to convert the old granary, now no longer needed for grain, into two bedrooms. The structure was warm, dry and well built, because the grain had to be kept from damp. It was raised on mushroom-shaped staddle stones, and the entrance was reached up a wooden stair. Under the tiled roof there was a door at each end: a big door above the steps at the inner end, and a two-leaved stable door at the outer end, over the lane, where sacks could be unloaded from a wagon below. Down one side of the central walkway the space was divided by curved wooden partitions into two bays, subdivided by wooden walls just low enough for a child to clamber over. Because it was so old, the movement of the grain and the constant friction of the sacks had polished the solid wooden partitions to satiny smoothness. The only thing like a window was the upper half of the stable door over the lane, and the outlook over the distant hills on a fine morning lifted the heart.

For me, the consequence of the move was that my journey to school now began at 7 o'clock with a three-mile walk through lonely lanes to the nearest station, where I caught the train for the half-hour ride to Guildford, followed by a mile walk from the station to the school. Eventually I acquired a rickety old bicycle to ride to the station. In the winter this meant leaving home before the sun rose and arriving home long after dark, so I could never take part in any leisure activities in Guildford, or meet friends outside school, except occasionally in the summer holidays. There were compensations in the pleasure of walking and cycling through beautiful quiet countryside and enjoying the wild flowers and bird song, which meant so much to me, undisturbed by the sound of traffic. Much as I loved the beautiful countryside and the freedom to wander, I did sometimes envy my school friends who lived in town.

Such a long journey to school had its effect on one's work. Breakfast was before seven, school dinners not til one, and it was nearly six by the time I got home for tea. After we moved to Little Prestwick Farm and had that difficult journey to school, we were always hungry and always tired. I wonder how much better we might have done at school had the circumstances of our lives been a little different.

In the spring of 1932, shortly after I entered sixth form, I had an unexpected adventure: participation in a weekend residential conference at St Hugh's College, Oxford, run by the League of Nations Union. The Union offered three free places to schools as prizes in a national essay competition. We were encouraged to enter by our enthusiastic history teacher, Miss Underwood, and remarkably, GCS gained all three prize places. The lectures and discussions were interesting, but the most memorable part of the weekend was living in college and exploring Oxford before breakfast and whenever we had an opportunity.

Early on Easter Morning the city was simply clamorous with bells from about six in the morning. Awakened by the bells, we three girls

Rainbow children off to school
From left to right: Ruth, Hilary, Rosemary, Geoffrey

got up and went out. There were no cars to be seen. I did think how wonderful it would be to be a university student, but such a thing was beyond my wildest dreams. University was really for wealthy young men, or so I thought.

The staff at GCS had other ideas. They hoped that I would be their first pupil to go to university, and they encouraged me to sit for the scholarship exams for several universities. They even intended that I should try for an Oxford scholarship, something for which I hardly dared to hope. In the summer of 1934, I sat the entrance examination for Reading University; the school told me they were putting me in for it 'for practice'. I spent an enjoyably social weekend in Reading, which included a written exam and interviews. While I was waiting to hear how I had done, I sat the London University Intercollegiate examinations which involved spending a day in London, doing English and Latin papers.

Almost immediately, I received two offers of scholarships, from Reading and from London, specifically for Bedford College, a women's college. Living in London, my native city, naturally appealed to me, and Bedford College offered the larger scholarship, so, somewhat regretfully, I turned my back on Reading and accepted the place at London.

When the letter arrived to tell me I had got the scholarship, our old postman noticed the London University stamp on the big envelope. The landlord's wife, learning from the postman that we had a letter from London University, asked my mother about it. Mother proudly told her that I had won a scholarship to Bedford College. 'Oh, how very nice for you, Mrs Rainbow,' responded Mrs Jackson. 'Thank goodness none of my girls will ever have to do that kind of thing!'

Learning Curve

Chapter 4

Flower of Cities All

I returned in 1934 to the city of my birth – London, the 'Flower of Cities all' as Dunbar, the Scottish poet, called it. When I arrived at Bedford College in October 1934, I was not in strange territory, but I was facing a new and quite unfamiliar life. I had won two scholarships and a grant to help me finance my studies. I was fully aware of how lucky I was; few women of my generation had the opportunity to attend college, and those who did were often from academic or professional families, with the resources to help them.

I loved being at Bedford. I enjoyed the delightful surroundings, the library and the academic staff. It was a small college, about six hundred students or so, and had the great advantage of small departments, small class sizes and a good deal of personal contact with the academic staff. In the English department I remember with special gratitude Kathleen Tillotson, slender and with a thick mass of auburn hair, who taught Chaucer and Middle English and was later famous as an authority on Dickens; the young John Butt, very tall and thin, whose life was devoted to Alexander Pope and baroque music; and Una Ellis-Fermor, a small, intense woman with visionary blue eyes who lectured on Elizabethan and Jacobean drama, the Irish Romantics, Ibsen and above all Christopher Marlowe, with whom she seemed to have an almost psychic connection. My early passion for Old English did not long survive the boring lectures of Professor P. G. Thomas.

Outside my own department, I had an unusual opportunity to hear the interesting philosophy lectures of Susan Stebbing, the author of *Thinking to Some Purpose*. Susan Stebbing was probably the member of the academic staff that I admired the most. A slow, awkward figure, subject to Menières Disease, she was nevertheless the best lecturer I ever heard. She never used a note, and ideas seemed to come to her fresh-minted to her as she spoke.

I lived in Bedford College House in Swiss Cottage, one of two or three big old houses that had been turned into student residences. To get to our lectures, we walked over Primrose Hill, through Regent's Park and the length of the boating lake, to the college gardens adjoining the Inner Circle. Nearby was the open-air theatre, newly established. We would be reminded of its presence by a distant sennet of trumpets at odd moments during lectures. The almost idyllic Regent's Park hardly seemed part of a great busy city. Outside, on London's roads, traffic was less than now, but there were still horrendous jams in the busy parts, with buses and lorries mingling with horse-drawn milk floats, coal carts and brewers' wagons, and with no traffic lights or any other form of control beyond policemen on point duty. The art of keeping traffic on the move was still in its infancy. London was turning into a modern city before our eyes. There were increasing numbers of double-decker buses with open tops, manned by drivers, and conductors equipped with punches who collected fares, announced the stops and kept order. Some women conductors were also employed, and were popularly known as 'clippies'. The Underground railway was very efficient, but I seldom used it. I enjoyed going to the theatre, but after saving up for tickets, my friends and I would save money by walking some miles to get to the theatre. We would regularly walk down from Primrose Hill to Sadlers Wells, the Old Vic, or the Tavistock Little Theatre, where we saw plays by Shaw and modern foreign playwrights such as Karel Capek.

When I went up to college, I had very few clothes that were appropriate to college life. My Aunt Muriel took me to the Haymarket, where she bought me a very fine sage green Burberry suit, which I wore constantly.

At Bedford, we had a small literary society, which invited interesting speakers including Stephen Spender and Vita Sackville-West. She spoke on the topic *Is it Still a Disadvantage to be a Woman?* As she strode onto the stage, a tall, striking woman in a severe black suit and a huge black sombrero, I was irresistibly reminded of a line from Ben Jonson, and whispered in the ear of my neighbour, 'How like to Anti-Christ thou lookst in that lewd hat!' It ran all along the line, and she was greeted with hilarity, which she seemed to enjoy. Quite unofficially we also had occasional political speakers, thanks to Peter and Jean Floud, a

From Lorna's student file at Bedford College

couple of young married students who made it their mission to reach out to Bedford. Our college was particularly isolated, as we had no students living at home who could bring outside elements into college life. In this we were very different from many of the big cities that had universities, like Manchester and Birmingham.

My fellow students and I had fairly quiet social lives. Often we would gather for mugs of cocoa, sitting on a divan in someone's room, and discuss our work, or college gossip, or issues of the day. There was less focus on men than one might expect; many of the students came to Bedford College from girls' schools, and were used to the cloistered nature of academic life. I had several particular friends, including another English student, Mary Rickwood, and the two of us became known as 'Rick and Ray'.

While I was still living at home, Father had hosted one or two farm students who would gain experience working with an established farmer before taking on their own farm. One of these was Bill, son of a well-to-do Scottish landed family, and a good many years older than I. He was a pleasant man who joined in our family conversations in the evening. After he returned to Scotland, my family kept in touch with him by post.

While I was attending Bedford, I received a letter from Bill, saying that he would be in London – would I like to have lunch with him? We met for lunch at a very nice restaurant, far grander than I had expected. We talked about what we had been doing since we last saw each other.

Eventually he asked, 'What are you doing after college? Do you ever think about being a farmer's wife?'

I had had enough of farm life in my own family, and told him decidedly that I intended to pursue an academic or a teaching career. It was only later that I recognized that this was his tentative approach to a discussion of marriage. I was sorry that I had not recognized this as we were talking, as he deserved a better response, but my answer would have been the same; I had no interest in returning to life on a farm.

I used to go home over the holidays, and in the rather cramped conditions at Prestwick Farm it was always difficult to stay on top of my academic work. The farm was a long way from any public library, and so Auntie Phyl, who commuted to London every day, brought me books from Westminster Library. Perhaps I was not grateful enough that she took on that extra chore on top of a long day's work.

There were three big preoccupations of student life in the 1930s, even in the Bedford backwaters. The big events that affected students like me were the dreadful economic situation with the consequent hunger marches, the crisis in the monarchy that led to the abdication of Edward VIII, and the Spanish Civil War.

In the mid-thirties, the economic Depression was severe. Many companies continued to reduce their work force, or shut down completely. There was some public assistance, but it was means-tested, so those that were out of work had to dispose of nearly everything in their homes, including rugs and some furnishings, before they would be given assistance.

At home, we had been very conscious of what was going on in the wider world. On my visits to London I had seen dreadful poverty and dreadful slums – undernourished children in the streets in ragged clothes. At Bedford I was aware that some of my fellow students came from big industrial towns, and in particular, I heard about conditions in Newcastle on Tyne and the north from Mary Rickwood. She found it hard to believe that I, coming from a beautiful area of the southern English countryside, could know anything about poverty or hardship. There was general awareness of poverty and unemployment in the industrial cities, but the plight of country people was masked by the fact that they lived in scattered communities and were rarely organized in unions. Nevertheless a considerable proportion of the nation's workforce laboured on the land and their trouble was no less real.

Jarrow, a town near Newcastle, was suffering from over seventy percent unemployment, due to closure of shipbuilding yards. A petition to Parliament was organized, asking that jobs be found for the men of Jarrow. A group of 200 men marched to London, to deliver the petition and to draw attention to high unemployment throughout the country. The march started in October of 1936, and the men marched ten or fifteen miles a day, going from town to town, and attracting much publicity. Often the marchers were greeted by crowds, and offered food, drink, and a place to rest. Some of us at Bedford followed the course of the march, also called the Jarrow Crusade, in the papers and as it neared London, we went out to stand by the roadside as the men passed and contribute whatever we could. The march was very well organized; many of the men were ex-servicemen who marched in good order, and were very dignified.

Parliament accepted the petition, but refused to meet representatives of the marchers, and took no action to improve the situation in Jarrow, leaving many people angry and disillusioned.

This attitude of the authorities in Britain goes some way to explain the growing influence of Communism at the time, especially among the young. A strong left-wing tendency was engendered by the rise of Nazi and Fascist regimes in Europe, of which our government seemed all too tolerant, and the very effective Soviet propaganda, which at that time was quite brilliant. I remember the illustrated magazines in our common room, full of bonny girls and handsome men tossing sheaves and driving tractors. They were attractive as well as interesting, and such a contrast to the desperate economic plight at home. At the time, many intellectuals, influenced by unimpeachable academics like Sidney and Beatrice Webb, thought Communism had the answers. The Left Book Club was widely influential, and shone a bright light on the parlous state of our own economy. We were reacting in part to a right-wing point of view, which was absolutely embedded in the middle classes at the time.

Back at Little Prestwick Farm, Father recounted how he had met our landlord and his wife on the road shortly before an election. She said, 'I suppose you're voting in the election, and that we can count on your vote?' Father responded shortly, 'I'm sorry – the ballot is secret. I don't tell anyone which way I vote.' It had to be secret. Farm labourers feared that they might be turned out of their cottages if they were known to have voted the 'wrong way'.

A crisis in the monarchy during this period introduced further uncertainty in a country that was already feeling great unrest. King George V was seen as a conservative, authoritarian figure, unlikely to be of any assistance to the working people. The Prince of Wales – the future Edward VIII – was surprisingly popular, particularly among the working classes. He had good public relations instincts, as well as clever advisors, and he benefitted from the contrast with his stiff and conventional parents. He did have something that might be called 'the common touch', but he was very much a playboy, and was in no way a democrat or even seriously committed to public welfare; he may even have been a crypto-Fascist.

Shortly before the death of King George V there was concern about his health across the country, and in college we were following the drama with interest. One day I was going to a lecture, carrying my pen and a bottle of ink, when I was caught in a swing door. The bottle of ink broke and made black stains on my sage green Burberry suit. All the dry cleaners could suggest was to dye the suit black, which they duly did. The first day I wore it was to a seminar on the day the King died. We were called into the office of the Head of English to hear the announcement on the radio. We greeted this broadcast in shocked silence, and one of my fellow students, looking at my sober black suit, whispered 'Lorna – how did you *know*?'

The Prince of Wales was now Edward VIII and behind the scenes, a constitutional crisis developed. Edward planned to marry an American woman, Mrs Simpson, who had been divorced. Stories about his private life did not get into the newspapers in the way that such news would now, though his affair with Mrs Simpson was well known among the British aristocracy, as well as in some countries overseas, especially after he went on a Mediterranean cruise with her in the summer of 1936.

As King of England, Edward was also the Head of the Church of England. Mrs Simpson, who had two ex-husbands living, was seen by the Church hierarchy as an unsuitable wife and Queen. There were lengthy negotiations between Edward and the Government, but eventually the options came down to two: either the King must give up Mrs Simpson, or he must abdicate. The British public followed this with great concern and anxiety: Edward VIII had been popular as Prince of Wales, it was hoped that he would modernize the monarchy, and it was unclear whether there could be an orderly succession if he abdicated.

In December of 1936, the Head of the English Department called us again into his office, and solemnly announced that we were going to listen to an important broadcast. We gathered around the wireless set, and heard the King announce his abdication:

You must believe me when I tell you that I have found it impossible to carry the heavy burden of responsibility and to discharge my duties as King as I would wish to do, without the help and support of the woman I love.

It was very shocking, and we felt as though the world was falling around us. The succession, which seemed such a well-understood and clear process, had been overturned. It made everything feel uncertain. Edward VIII was succeeded by his brother, George VI, and was given the title of Duke of Windsor.

Students and their teachers were deeply concerned with left-wing politics at this time, and not only at home. The outbreak in 1936 of the Spanish Civil War between the Fascist forces of Franco and the Socialist government moved us greatly. I attended a packed meeting to support the Spanish Republican cause, held in the Albert Hall, at which the Duchess of Atholl – the 'Red Duchess' – spoke movingly on behalf of the International Brigades. A collection was taken for medical supplies for Spain; since I had no spare cash, I took off my gold bracelet and dropped it into the bucket.

The Duchess, so uncharacteristic of the aristocracy, was a most exciting and effective speaker for the anti-Fascist cause. It was extraordinary how many male students abandoned their studies and set off for Spain to join the International Brigades. We invited one or two of them to talk to informal meetings at Bedford College. Though many of us cared passionately about the cause, we felt very cut off from the outside world, both because of the isolated setting in which we lived, and because as women, there seemed to be so much less that we could do to help.

Looking back, I can see that the Thirties were very much a hinge period, marking the start of a new era which would take some years to develop. Some of the biggest changes were concerned with women and family relationships. The well-defined roles of men and women were evolving, and women's horizons were becoming less limited as new technologies made running a household easier and family planning began to advance.

The relationship of people to the countryside was slowly changing, too. The poverty-stricken but beautiful countryside of my childhood, with its flowers and birds, its night skies full of stars, its rusty gates, and the naturally self-sustaining cycle of farms, was coming to an end. Farm horses, which reproduced themselves and fed from the land, were being replaced by tractors. The change from horses to tractors for farm work altered the nature of farming. Horses were adaptable, could be used in a variety of circumstances, and were, in a way, self-sustaining. You had to feed a horse, but their droppings could be used for fertilizer, and they could produce young to replace themselves. Tractors required imported fuel, and changed the landscape. Since they were most effective on large tracts of land, hedges were rooted out, and the size of farms increased to introduce greater efficiencies. Tractors were noisy, tending to further isolate the workers who drove them. The small family operated dairy farms in which the animals were regarded as living creatures, not as production units, would soon be seen as too inefficient to feed the growing population.

I came to see my choice of Bedford College as perhaps unfortunate. It had high standards, excellent tutors, and a long and fine tradition. It was also the first UK College to award degrees to women. Alas, it was so small, so isolated, like a very high-class finishing school for young ladies. Earnest and enclosed, it resembled nothing so much as the high-minded society of *Love's Labour's Lost*. It was, I think, an outmoded concept. Its doom was sealed later on when – instead of being greatly enlarged and opened to men students – it was absorbed into another women's college and virtually obliterated. It would have been so much better, I realized later, to have gone to a mixed university. At the time, however, I knew only that I had reached university against all the odds, and I enjoyed my education enormously. I remain very grateful to Bedford.

Some of my tutors were convinced that I would take a First in English, and go on to an academic career. A First is hard to get, but the opportunities for postgraduate research were very scarce indeed, so it was important to have one. There were very few fellowships or studentships available, but there was an endowment for postgraduate students for which I was encouraged to apply. Sadly, when the results were announced, I had only achieved an Upper Second.

Most people are pleased to get a good Upper Second, but I felt that the end of the world had come. I had been persuaded by the English Department to set my sights on an academic career, but now my hopes were shattered. Some of the English staff seemed to be avoiding me, perhaps unsure of what to say; their avoidance added to my distress. The final blow was the discovery that this was the 'off year' for the postgraduate endowment, and the money would not be available until the following year.

When I was feeling at my lowest, I found in my pigeon hole a little note from the philosophy professor, Susan Stebbing, saying, 'Dear Miss Rainbow, do not be distressed by having got an Upper Second. I never found it the slightest disadvantage.' What could be kinder?

I graduated from Bedford College in 1937, and thought, 'Whatever shall I do now?' Jobs were hard to come by, and the Depression was still omnipresent. I wondered if I might take a university librarianship course, but no grants were available. Then I thought that perhaps I could raise some money and go to secretarial college. Being a graduate secretary might open up some interesting possibilities. Auntie Phyl warned me against this plan. She said I would never be able to escape from a secretarial role, and should always be in a subordinate position to some man whose grammar I might well have to correct.

I was in despair. There were really so few opportunities for an educated woman at the time, but I had to earn my living somehow. My last resort seemed to be a teacher-training course.

I was lucky enough to get a place at a graduate teacher-training college in Cambridge, starting in September of 1937, and obtained a local authority grant to pay for it. I had revised my plans: I would become an English teacher, like my admired Miss Dawes at Guildford County School for Girls, and would follow in her footsteps.

Chapter 5

Quiet Flows the Cam

How fortunate I was! I would spend a whole year in Cambridge, in a college dedicated to the training of graduate women teachers. The college was small, with fifty or sixty students, and enjoyed a high academic reputation, but had no connection with the university, which then had no education department. Pleasantly situated at some distance from the town centre, the college was quiet, and many of its study bedroom windows had an excellent view of Fenner's, the university cricket ground. It was an isolated community, but a delightful place to live and study.

The course of studies was full of interesting subjects: theories of education from Plato to the present; comparative education in different countries; the history of education in Britain; child development and psychology; intelligence testing, a subject then recently developed by Jean Piaget and much discussed by psychologists and education experts; statistics, which I enjoyed though I had never much liked maths at school; and more practical matters such as lesson planning. All of these topics were covered in the lecture-room.

Practical training was more of a problem, both for the college and for us. At this time, nearly a decade before the 1944 Butler Act, secondary education was not obligatory for all children, and the number of secondary schools, especially for girls, was very limited. Cambridge was then quite a small town, and the county of Cambridge had few towns of any size. Even though the number of student teachers was small, it was extremely hard to find suitable girls' schools where they could be placed for teaching practice. The usual pattern in other training colleges was to attach each student teacher to a school for several weeks, or even a term, to provide an immersion course in practical education. The plan at the Cambridge college was weaker – for students to spend one day a week in a school, with no continuity or sense of involvement.

The school to which I was assigned was an expensive private boarding school. The classes were typically ten pupils or fewer, and the girls, even if bored, were charmingly polite and beautifully behaved. This school was in the rural countryside, at some considerable distance from Cambridge. There was no bus service, and the school was too far away for me to cycle, so on school practice days my tutor would drive me there in the morning, and back again after school. At lunchtime we would eat sandwiches in a nearby field or in the car. My tutor's day was not altogether wasted as she always brought essays to mark or reading to catch up on, but I cannot believe this system would have survived even the most cursory cost–benefit analysis. All of this, however interesting, did nothing to prepare me for the shock of real life in a tough mixed school in a Midlands industrial town, a few months later.

Meanwhile there was a great deal to enjoy in Cambridge. In my leisure time, I explored the countryside on my new Raleigh bicycle, a generous present from Auntie Muriel and Uncle Aubrey. It was the first new bicycle I had ever owned. I went to the Cambridge School of Art, where our college encouraged us to take optional courses. I did a course in bookbinding, which I loved. I also joined a life class, since I had always been enthusiastic about drawing. Sometimes I would go to the Dot, a Cambridge café, and sketch professors as they passed through. My friends recognized these eminences from my sketches.

I worked hard and attentively in my life class, and after a time my charcoal studies on white paper had warm approval from the art-school tutor. I took the best of the pictures back to college to pin up on the walls of my study-bedroom. They covered quite a lot of space. Then one day a visit to the college by a minor royal was announced. It was to be a most important occasion: the college must be in perfect order, and we students must all be immaculate in every detail. The bursar made an anxious last-minute tour of the whole building, and when she reached my room she was appalled by all the male and female nudes. They were very decorous, but they had to come down.

A dominant presence in Cambridge was the English don, Dr Frank Leavis. He was a Fellow of Downing College, but despite – or perhaps because of – his controversial reputation, he had no university appointment. He had founded a critical journal called *Scrutiny*, which was influential and independent in its views and was widely read. It provided a launch pad for several young academics and clever students who later became very successful. Someone told me that Leavis's lectures were always crowded, and that it was easy to get in as nobody checked entrants at the lecture-room door. So I gate-crashed, and found myself in a throng of enthusiastic students, with no girls as far as I could see. Leavis himself was fortyish, lean and athletic looking – I learnt later that he would be out most mornings to run in the Gog Magog hills – and was less formally dressed than was usual for academics.

The lecture was exhilarating, lively, fresh and direct. It was like hearing a clever man thinking aloud and sharing thoughts as they came to him. At the end, he invited anyone present who wished to send him a short essay, unsigned, on any topic that seemed relevant to them. He hoped for a wide variety of examples of ideas that it might be interesting to discuss. Though I had not planned to, I did write a short essay and left it rather furtively in his pigeonhole. Strangely, I remember it very well: it was about A.E. Housman's *Shropshire Lad*, the use of the first person, and the difference between sympathy and empathy. No doubt it was my acquaintance with real farm labourers – so unlike Housman's – that commended the subject to me.

In his lecture the week after, Dr Leavis talked about the many essays he had received, and quoted from some of them. Then he read mine aloud, and asked the 'chap' who had written it to come to see him later. I should have been too shy, except that I could not let pass the assumption that I was a chap. The result was a friendly invitation to tea at his house.

This was the beginning of my membership in the small circle of Leavis's disciples who met for weekly tea-drinking and earnest discussion. On my first visit, the formidably clever Mrs Queenie Leavis greeted me, saying she was glad to see a girl after all these young men. I also made the acquaintance of their precocious small son, who showed me the contents page of a literary journal, and pointed to his friends' names, including T.S. Eliot and Ezra Pound.

I enjoyed these meetings and felt privileged to be there. I also felt intimidated by all the clever young men who had read so much more than I had, in several languages, and who seemed so knowledgeable and sure of themselves. I came to dislike the intolerant and self-congratulatory tone that sometimes coloured the discussions. I wished I could be as sure of *anything* as they seemed to be of *everything*. No doubt they wondered, 'Why is she here?'

Sometimes when the teatime meetings dispersed, Leavis would invite me to stay a while for another pot of tea and a little quiet conversation, and then he would walk me back to my college. I have a vivid mental picture of one such occasion, with Frank Leavis, that hardy man, striding coatless out of his front door, in an open-necked shirt and pullover, while snowflakes were falling around us.

I greatly admired Leavis. He might have been too doctrinaire, too combative and sometimes tactless, and was sometimes sharply critical of academic colleagues; he referred to one of them, without fail, as 'the egregious Hen!' But he was a man of honesty and integrity, who cared about standards, and who was determined to uphold them regardless of comfort, popularity or personal advantage. I admired him for all this, and for his spare writing. If his words blew harshly through the universities, his cleansing wind was probably exactly what 'Eng. Lit.' needed at that time.

The happiest experience of all during my Cambridge year was musical. Soon after I arrived, I found my way to the Cambridge University Music Society (CUMS), auditioned for the choir, and was accepted as a second soprano. The director and conductor of CUMS was Dr Boris Ord of King's College, a brilliant musician and a very hard taskmaster. He was especially hard on the women singers, but his sarcasm did not discourage us or lessen our devotion. CUMS became the great joy of my life.

Choral singing was a different experience in the thirties. Now that there is such an enormous range of recorded music easily available, it must be quite unusual for any choir to begin learning a new work without ever having heard it before. In the thirties, picking up a new score probably meant the exploration of virgin territory for most of us. It so happened that a few days before CUMS did the *Verdi Requiem*, there was a wireless broadcast of a performance conducted by Toscanini, and Boris told us not to miss it. We gathered in various little groups around whatever wireless sets we could find. This was the first time that many of us had heard it. It is not a piece that I now greatly like, but it was very exhilarating.

A more astonishing pleasure was in store. One day, Boris told us that we were going to learn a piece that might have been performed once, over 300 years ago, but had not been performed since. We divided into eight small choirs of five voices, each with its own hand-written part-books, and we rehearsed separately until the final rehearsal. We studied our parts, and learnt to count what seemed like endless bars of silence, practising in our small, separate choirs in Boris's rooms in King's. On the morning of the performance, we assembled for the first and last rehearsal of *Spem in Alium,* and heard all our voices gathered together in the single splendour of Tallis's great forty-part motet.

Perhaps Boris Ord was able to imagine it, but for the rest of us the Tallis project was an adventure into the unknown. I could not have imagined a motet in forty parts: for me, Handel's choruses were the limit of choral complexity. Nor did the name Tallis mean anything more to me then than a vague memory of a solemn old hymn tune. This long-forgotten composition by an ancient church musician might, I thought, be a brilliant and eccentric exercise in technical virtuosity – perhaps interesting, but not beautiful or moving.

We sang the motet for an audience in King's College Chapel, and it was broadcast by the BBC. It was late afternoon, with innumerable candles flickering in the beautiful old building. I do not know what kind of impression it made on the audience or on the people who listened to the broadcast, but for me, and surely for all of us who sang it, this great Tallis motet was a revelation – a unique experience of overwhelming beauty and power. It starts with one voice, and then one voice after another comes in until it builds up to this enormous fugue, and then it all tails away again. It just dies away. It is thrilling to hear when it is well done. Of course, nobody can ever hear it the way we heard it, because we heard it for the first time as we were singing it. It was a day of perfect joy.

I had written to Mother and Father to tell them of the broadcast. The family listened devotedly on their old wireless. Mother wrote to me later about the thrilling solo entry and then the great wave of voices that sounded like the sea. It was an experience we all remembered – it was transcendental.

With examinations over, my time at Cambridge was coming to an end. What had it all been for? I looked back on a year that contained varied experiences, and one glorious event. I had met some interesting people but made no life-long friends. But what about the real purpose of my post-graduate course: to turn me from a young graduate with a BA Honours in English into a qualified secondary school teacher?

At the end of the year, the Principal of the college gathered us all together and gave us a pep talk. We were now equipped with professional training and degrees, she told us, and ready to engage with 'the cash nexus and the world of work'.

I was twenty-two years old, and about to start on my career. By this stage in their lives, the children I had known at the village school had been working for eight years, and some of my contemporaries from Guildford County School had been earning a living for six years. Some were even married with children. I, on the other hand, despite my age and my indispensable certificate, felt as though I was still not really grown up.

It was 1938, the Depression still hung over the country, and war seemed imminent. I applied for several secondary school teaching jobs, and received an offer from Belper, a North Midland industrial town, to teach English and Latin. The school was described as 'co-educational', which to me indicated a progressive educational programme. As I discovered, the school, although co-educational in name, was essentially segregated, with boys sitting on one side of the room, and girls on the other, as a simple cost-saving measure to teach more pupils. There were even separate entrances for boys and girls. If a boy misbehaved, he might be publicly humiliated by being sent to sit with the girls. No girl would ever have been sent to sit with the boys as a punishment.

The school itself was seriously overcrowded. There had been plans over the years to enlarge and rebuild it, but funds were lacking under the difficult economic conditions, so it was just old and crowded. Classes had as many as forty pupils, and there was a strong sense of just making do.

I soon realized how sheltered all my previous school experience had been. On my first day, I was in a class taking the register, when suddenly a bizarre figure blew in, looking like an ancient crow, with a great flapping musty old gown around him, and wild gray hair. He came rushing into the room and sat down next to me at the table.

Breathing stale tobacco fumes all over me, he said, 'You're going to help me with the Latin, I hear.' I said, 'Yes, yes, I believe I am going to be teaching some Latin.' 'Well,' he said, 'Can you take the sixth form for Virgil?' He kept edging his chair closer to mine, and eventually he got his arm around behind me. I moved my chair a bit, and by the end we were right at the end of the table and I could move my chair no further. The class, naturally, watched my confusion with glee; I was embarrassed to death, and unsure how to deal with this senior master.

The children of Belper were a long way from being the well-mannered girls of the private school where I had done my practice teaching. The boys were uncouth and boisterous and the girls seemed cowed. They spoke in a dialect that I often failed to understand.

In one class of 14-year-olds the set book was *Lorna Doone*. The girls drooled and sighed and wept their way through the romance of it, but the boys jeered. They only liked the fist-fight at the beginning and the frightful end of Carver Doone in the bog.

> *The black bog had him by the feet; the sucking of the ground drew him on, like the thirsty lips of death…*

I went to the senior English mistress to tell her the book was quite unsuitable for a mixed class of that age, but was told to 'Just get on with your work!' Some of the teachers there were quite cynical, and felt their job was simply to keep the children under control.

I was very naïve as a teacher. There was one bright boy, a German refugee called Eddie Eisner, who spoke very good English. One day I was correcting another boy's poor English, and I said, 'Don't make that mistake – why can't you speak like Eddie Eisner?' It was a beginner's error on my part, to single out one boy as being superior, and especially a boy who was already an outsider. Eddie responded, 'Please, Miss Rainbow, it is easier for me. I had to learn English, not just pick it up'. It was hard to learn how to teach, when there was no coaching or help.

Many years later, I was attending a meeting of the Royal Society, where a middle-aged professor stood and asked a question, identifying himself as Professor Edward Eisner. We spoke briefly after the meeting, and, amazingly, after nearly half a century, he recognized me as 'Miss Rainbow' from Belper School.

Teaching at Belper was not a happy experience. I boarded locally, but there was no choral group or other activities for me to participate in. I made a few friends, but in general it was lonely. I would exchange letters with my family, but I do not think they had any sense of how difficult this life was for me.

When World War II started in September of 1939, the school soon faced a shortage of staff, since male teachers were being called up for military service. At the same time, the Belper district was designated as a reception area for a boys' prep school from Southsea, since it was considered rural and remote. This was a strange decision, since the Rolls Royce factory, not far away at Derby, made a likely target for German air raids. Because there were only enough classrooms for one school, the two schools operated a 'hot-desking' system, as well as using some overflow capacity in local halls. Students had to take their books home every night, and inevitably many books were missing when needed.

As the Southsea students arrived, the school started to overflow all over the town, and classes were held in the town hall and in church halls and chapels. There I found myself in vocal competition with the obnoxious Latin master. Bellowing like the Old Testament's Bull of Bashan, he taught Latin to a class of thirty-five, while I taught English to a class of similar size on the other side of the hall. I even taught in the old Workhouse infirmary chapel, with the children sitting in pews and me standing in the pulpit, trying to teach the poor little creatures about essay writing, with no desks for them to write on. Was it really true, or did I dream that I once taught there with the coffin of a deceased inmate on the steps behind me?

While I did my best to teach under such circumstances, I felt helpless and unhappy. Despite my teaching certificate, I was quite unprepared for the job, as my training was far more about the theory of teaching than the practice of it. The only teaching I enjoyed was of the sixth form, where the students were bright and dedicated, and the level of discussion was adult. I might have survived or even been happy in a school more like GCS, but I do not think that even the great Miss Dawes would have thrived in Belper. I certainly did not.

I began to have fainting fits. My doctor diagnosed heart problems, which required a complete rest to allow me to recover my strength. In 1940, I returned home to the family farm at Prestwick and later resigned my post in Belper, never to return to teaching. My parents, who had had such high hopes for their eldest daughter with her degree and career, now hid their disappointment to give me their time and attention. With my poor health, I felt that I had added to their burdens with this failure.

Aunt Muriel and Uncle Aubrey invited me to come and recuperate with them. They had left their London home, which was later destroyed in the Blitz, and were living out the war in a hotel in Lynmouth, Devon. The hotel was in a lovely location, overlooking a rapidly flowing rocky river, shaded by trees, which ran down to Lynmouth Harbour. When I arrived, I was so weak that I could not walk the half-mile to the harbour without a rest, but after two or three months I became much stronger.

The country was totally engaged in the war, and I determined to join the WRENS as soon as I was medically fit. Before this could happen, however, I received a letter from Una Ellis-Fermor, who was by then based in Cambridge. She had heard of my situation, and knew of vacancies in the Cambridge offices of the Ministry of Pensions. I secured a clerical job there, and on fifty shillings a week I was able to pay rent and live independently in Cambridge.

In my spare time, I did part-time lecturing for adult education classes, as did Bernard Blackstone (later a professor at the University of Beirut.), a post-graduate whom I had never met. As winter drew on we shared a taxi, travelling through the blackout to and from our respective villages, where we taught. We could not see each other, and we did not converse, but out of the dark came a solemn voice reciting canto after canto of Dante in fluent Italian. One day he materialized; he invited me to coffee in his rooms and the mysterious voice acquired a human form.

I had not been in Cambridge long when I received a telegram from the Ministry of Labour and National Service in London. It was tracing recent graduates not already working for the war effort and not accounted for. I was instructed to report to the War Office for an interview the following week.

On His Majesty's Service

Chapter 6

London

I turned into Whitehall and passed the modest statue of Charles I on my way to the War Office. This square stone building with its little turret at each corner seemed enormous to me, though it was far smaller than the big Ministry of Defence building which was later built next door to it. Still, compared to the organisations I had known hitherto – my school, the two colleges in London and Cambridge, and the Derbyshire grammar school – it was impressively large. I went up the stone steps into a high-ceilinged entrance hall with panelled walls and a marble floor. Everywhere there were men in uniform, not a woman in sight. I went to the reception desk and soon an elderly, black-clad messenger escorted me up a wide staircase to the second floor. This was the Principal floor where all the top brass had their offices. He ushered me into a large room with tall windows and a big fireplace, and introduced me to the Brigadier, a stocky middle-aged officer sitting at a massive mahogany desk.

His manner was brisk but courteous, and he spoke authoritatively. The War Office, he told me, was adapting very rapidly to meet wartime demands. One innovation was a new unit called the Army Council Secretariat (ACS), modelled on the War Cabinet Secretariat, but, he hoped, even better organised. The ACS would serve the Army Council, the internal high level committees, and, jointly with the Cabinet Office, many important inter-departmental committees. It would become the central repository for the records of government decisions.

The Brigadier then outlined various kinds of secretariat work, which were all new to me, and explained that the post I was being considered for was that of a Junior Administrative Assistant (JAA). This was a new grade, created for women, as a wartime expedient in the three Service departments, and it was expected that they would be few in number. The Service departments had not employed women before, certainly not in the administrative class. It was equivalent to the Assistant Principal (AP) post, but there was no promotion grade above JAA, as there was for the APs.

The Army Council Secretariat, he told me, was a select group of which the highest standards were expected, and the work was extremely exacting. If I were accepted into it, much would be demanded of me, and I must be prepared to work hard. At the end of the interview, the Brigadier said, 'Start next week.' I had been accepted.

When I arrived for work on that first day, I was assigned to a stout friendly pink-faced staff Colonel. His main responsibility was a small expert committee, which was conducting a thorough examination, branch by branch, of functions and procedures within the War Office. This committee had been set up by the dynamic Permanent Under-Secretary, Sir James Grigg. A small team of businessmen and academics visited each branch to study its functions and conduct working practice reviews, and remained long enough to observe the flows. In this way, they brought to light many instances where duplication of effort could be removed, procedures speeded up or even eliminated, efficiency improved, and economies effected. Through this committee, Sir James was able to bring radical reform into the War Office without interfering with the urgent business of running the War.

All this was an extraordinary new world, utterly remote from any of my earlier experiences. Now I was in a big, complex, powerful, and almost entirely masculine organisation, dealing with huge issues. There was so much to learn and I was woefully ignorant. No wonder I felt quite bewildered. What did all these initials mean – VCIGS, AG, GSO, MI3, KR, ACI, PUS, AUS[1]?

Though the pace was hectic, there was no clear way for me to contribute. The regular Army Colonel for whom I worked had no idea what I was there for. I was an unknown quantity: I had no office

---

[1] For the curious: VCIGS – Vice Chief of the Imperial General Staff, AG – Adjutant General , GSO – General Staff Office, MI3 – War Office, Military Intelligence 3, KR – King's Regulations, ACI – Army Council Instruction, PUS – Permanent Undersecretary, AUS – Assistant Undersecretary

experience, I knew nothing about the Army, and I knew nothing about the War, beyond what any intelligent reader would know from newspapers. He just did not know what on earth I was supposed to do. I used to sit there waiting for him to give me something to do, and thinking, 'I must make myself useful.' Then he would ask me to fetch some more stationery, or ask the porter for a cup of tea. I was running around like his little messenger girl, feeling very frustrated.

Then I was asked to attend the meetings of a committee which was to examine and advise on difficult problems of status and working conditions in the various women's auxiliary services – the ATS, which was a women's military service, and FANYs, QAIMNS, and VADs[2], all of which were volunteer organizations. These women's services had different traditions, privileges, and ranks, which led to some resentment when their staffs served in the same facility. The committee was trying to iron out these anomalies, without destroying the traditions of each group. I was told to make myself useful to the committee, which at first meant scheduling rooms for meetings, and acting as general gofer. There were three distinguished women members: the beautiful Lady Mountbatten, head of the St John Ambulance Brigade, Lady Limerick from the British Red Cross, and Mary Stocks, an academic and well-known writer and broadcaster. Mary Stocks took over as chair of the committee from Sir Walter Elliott, MP, when he broke his leg and was out of action. She was an excellent chair. I became more involved over time, and accompanied Lady Limerick and Lady Mountbatten on their tours of barracks and hospitals to review work conditions, but I remained a general factotum.

I tried to learn all I could. I read assiduously all the daily circulation folders containing the ACS correspondence, briefs, telegrams, minutes, and papers of the previous day, and my Colonel seemed satisfied. I filled in any spare time by studying books on the history of the War Office and other great departments of state, on the development of Cabinet government, and on Lord Hankey's creation of the Cabinet Secretariat and its techniques.

––––––––––––––––––––

[2] ATS – Auxiliary Territorial Service, FANYs - First Aid Nursing Yeomanry, QAIMNS - Queen Alexandra's Imperial Military Nursing Service, VADs - Volunteer Aid Detachments

I read the journal *Public Administration* avidly, and realized that the present war was inadvertently becoming a giant Organization and Methods (O&M) laboratory. Management studies, I learnt from the Brigadier, were providing a new body of theory that was going to be very useful and important. The work was being done by a team of experts based in Manchester. The Brigadier was well versed in O&M, both the theory and practice, and he would occasionally lend me current papers on the subject.

The War had an impact on my whole family. Father decided that he wanted to join up, though he was over fifty years old. Most of the forces did not want someone of that age, but he was very patriotic and very determined, and finally joined the Pioneer Corps, which provided engineering support. He spent much of the War in Liverpool and other areas affected by bombing, helping to clear the rubble and bodies. Mother remained on the farm with the younger children, and continued to run it for a year. During this time, Granny died suddenly without any illness, and Auntie Phyl moved to London. Finally, Mother sold the livestock and equipment and moved the rest of the family to London, where she found an empty flat in Glyn Mansions in West Kensington. After nearly twenty years of working on the farm, Mother returned to office work, and though in her fifties, she became a junior clerk in the Ministry of Health.

When I first started working at the War Office, I just found digs wherever I could, but when Auntie Phyl left the farm, she and I moved into a small early Victorian house, one of a row of little houses built for senior servants at Kensington Palace who lived out. It was in Gordon Place, a very pretty cul-de-sac off Church Street, just behind St. Mary Abbott's Church. It would have been prohibitively expensive in ordinary times, but it had been left empty because the husband was in the armed forces, and his family were away in the country.

From our windows we could see – and hear! – the battery of anti-aircraft guns in nearby Kensington Gardens. I was a fire warden in our neighbourhood, equipped with tin hat, stirrup pump, and bucket of sand. After an air raid, I would sometimes deal with incendiaries lodged on our roof, or help cope with fires in neighbouring houses. We must have saved many empty homes from destruction.

Walking home from the War Office to our place in Kensington, I took a route that brought me through some of the great parks of London. I would head off through St. James's Park, then Green Park, then through Hyde Park, and finally through Kensington Gardens, a walk of several miles. It could be enjoyable to walk through the parks at the end of the day, but could also be hazardous. Sometimes I would encounter an Air Raid warden, who would warn the few pedestrians to get under cover, and I would promise that if anything came close, I would dive into a shelter. It was odd how accustomed you became to being bombed. Women walking alone also had to contend with lonely men. I remember once walking along a street after dark when a soldier fell into step with me and started talking to me. I tried to shake him off, but he was persistent, so I directed my steps towards a small church where I expected to find confessions being heard. I went in to the welcoming light of the votive candles and the door closed behind me. It was a tactic that I used more than once.

I had a very different sort of meeting with another young man. As I was walking home, he fell in step with me, and asked if he could speak with me. His face had a look of great distress; I suggested we get a cup of tea. Over tea in a Lyons shop he told me about his work; he was engaged in rescue operations, searching through rubble for the survivors of air raids and collecting the bodies of victims. The work had become unbearably distressing. We talked for a while and, hoping to distract him from his distress, I asked what he had done in civilian life.

He was a pacifist, which is why he was not in the armed forces. Before the War he had been a music student, a singer. 'I'm singing this weekend,' he said, 'at the YMCA. Would you like to come?' We talked for a few minutes more, and then went our separate ways. I did attend his concert that weekend, where he sang a Schumann song cycle very well, but I never saw him after that. The brief interaction did not seem strange at the time; there was an impermanent quality to much of life.

There were several narrow escapes during the Blitz. For a while, Father's half-sister Beatrice lived with me and Auntie Phyl at Gordon Place. Auntie Bea was in her sixties, very frail, and profoundly deaf. One evening she called out to me and said, 'I would like a cup of tea

London during WWII

and some toast, dear.' I went into the kitchen to prepare it, when quite suddenly there was an enormous explosion, quite close, and the front door blew open with a *swoosh*. A strong wind roared up the stairs, blowing dead leaves all through the house. All the lights went out, so I turned the gas off, and went off to look for candles. Then there was a plaintive little call from Auntie Bea, 'You're being a very long time with that tea and toast, dear.'

While Phyl and I lived at one end of Kensington High Street, Mother and the younger children were at the other end, perhaps a mile away. We decided to meet nightly at an air raid shelter that was between our homes, so we could be together, for good or for ill. The conditions in the air raid shelters were crowded and unpleasant, but they did provide protection. After one raid, Mother returned to her flat at Glyn Mansions to discover that all the windows of the flat had been blown out, and a long gleaming dagger of glass had pierced the mattress where she would have usually slept!

In May of 1941, I took a bus with my friend Dick Spann, on leave from his naval station, to go to a concert at Queen's Hall. There had been an air raid in the area the night before, and much of our route was badly damaged, so the bus had to crawl down unfamiliar streets. We felt sure we would be late, and I remarked 'Oh well, Queen's Hall may not be there by the time we finally arrive.' Sadly, it was not: it had been bombed the previous night. There was nothing left of it but rubble and the sound of dripping water.

At the War Office, my work changed and became more interesting and much more exacting. The Colonel for whom I had been working was moved elsewhere, and his place was taken by another officer who immediately began my education. Lieutenant-Colonel Alan Mocatta was just back from Burma, and was an impressive figure, tall and erect, radiating energy and vitality. With his thick black hair, large black eyes, and olive skin, he looked Hispanic rather than British. In fact, as I learnt later, his ancestors had fled Spain to escape persecution in the seventeenth century, when many Sephardic Jewish refugees had been given safe haven in England. He had been a barrister before the War, and in later life he became a High Court Judge.

He immediately gave me more demanding work. At first, I just proofread papers, and then I edited some of them. When he went to a meeting to do the minutes, I would come with him as a sort of backup, taking my own notes. One day, after we had gone to a high-powered inter-departmental meeting together, he said, 'You are doing the minutes this time.' I was doubtful, but he encouraged me, and assured me that he would help me, though only if necessary.

I will never forget dictating those first minutes, because it was such a mental effort. It took me quite a long time, and it must have been hard on the typist. By the time I had finished, I was wrung out with the effort. I gave the typed draft to Colonel Mocatta, who made a few corrections, and then it was ready to go.

When I commented on his kindness in taking so much trouble, he laughed and told me that it was not kindness, but a determination to get from me all I was able to deliver. After a while, we divided the committees up between us. It was a lot of work. I do not think anybody else in the secretariat did minutes quite the way we did, because we always dictated when we got back from the meeting, say at 5 o'clock, with a late-duty shorthand writer. We would dictate the minutes — complete with the punctuation, the tabulation, the underlining, the capitalization, and everything, so the duty typist knew exactly what to type — and finish them by half past six. They were then typed straight onto a stencil, run off on the mimeograph, and went out on the night courier. I do not think anybody else in the Secretariat worked at our speed. Our system took time and practice to develop, but that was how we liked to work.

Working with Colonel Mocatta was almost like having a first-rate Oxford tutor at your sole disposal every day. If I drafted a brief or a paper, he would sit down, go through it with me, and say, 'Why did you say that?' or 'What's the basis for that?' or 'Do you think you ought to explain this more fully?' or 'Is that the best way to express this?' He always encouraged me to think about who my readership was. I learned more from him in a short time than I could have learned from anybody in months or years. He taught me how to study documents in a new and often revealing way, a method which I later found invaluable in research.

In our spare time, or at lunch in the canteen, we talked of many other things besides work and the War. He lent me books on history, law, and philosophy, and suggested I should consider training as a lawyer. Of course we always addressed one another as Colonel Mocatta and Miss Rainbow, as was the custom in those days, and especially in the War Office environment. Then one day he asked me — very politely — if he might call me by my Christian name, and if I would call him Alan, though we did not do so outside our own office.

The ACS staff sometimes worked with our opposite numbers on the American military staff in London. There were joint proposals that had to be approved by both American and British officialdom, and sometimes the proposal stood a better chance of success if it came from the American side. On occasion, the Americans would ask us to draft it. We would write a proposal in American style, which they would then submit through their channels. That was a good challenge that we both greatly enjoyed.

Alan was the best of bosses, the best of teachers, and a much-valued friend until the end of his life. We kept in touch, and would meet occasionally for lunch in a favourite restaurant in Piccadilly. He wrote the kindest of letters when my first book, on British atomic weapons trials, was published in 1987, forty-five years after our War Office days. I worked with him for just two years, but it now seems a disproportionately long period of my life – two years of intense pressure and absorbing interest, and an education which was to be more valuable to me later than I could possibly have foreseen. Having Alan as a mentor was one of the most fortunate aspects of my war-time career; from him I learned ways of analysis and presentation that have been valuable to me throughout my life.

The joint directors of the ACS, the Brigadier and his civil servant colleague, ran a very efficient and well-integrated machine. At the end of each working day, the chief clerk would present them with folders containing copies of all the documents – drafts, letters, minutes, telegrams, and committee papers – created by the eight officers of the ACS staff that day. By nine o'clock next morning at the latest, the Brigadier had read everything and would begin his calls on members of staff, to comment or ask for more information. He was trenchant in his criticisms, but always generous in his appreciation of a good piece of work. Every day at about half past twelve he would hold a brief meeting in his office, and every ACS staff member attended to give an account of the work in hand, so that we were all aware of our colleagues' activities and could collaborate wherever appropriate.

This war period, for me and for many people of my age, seemed like a period of time out of time, bearing little relationship to before or after. For those of us who had no settled adult life to return to, the post-war future seemed distant and unreal, and our whole existence was concentrated in the extraordinary present. One strange aspect of life was that one became so used living in the midst of uncertainty and great danger. Even though I was in London during most of Blitz, and throughout the V1 and V2 bomb attacks, I never actually felt frightened. I knew that any night might be my last, but every morning I would wake up with new energy to the challenge of another day.

The Brigadier, who had my interests at heart, thought that I should take advantage of my position to look out for a suitable husband among the eligible well-bred young men around me on Whitehall. He gave me a few kindly hints. Colonel Stephenson's wife, he suggested, could help me with a good hairdresser and some clothes shopping; my accent was not *quite* right, but I spoke very nicely and was, he knew, a quick learner. I was grateful for his kindness, but was not convinced about his strategy for changing my life.

The ACS provided secretaries for high-level committees and jointly with the War Office for many inter-departmental committees. One especially interesting one dealt with Equipment for Patriot Forces, the resistance movements in occupied European countries. The Allies assisted these resistance groups in great secrecy. Allied agents were sent to encourage and assist them with information and communications, and by arranging for the provision of such equipment as small arms, ammunition, tools, ropes, medical supplies, books, radio sets, and clothing. The Equipment for Patriot Forces committee received secret messages with lists of requirements, arranged procurement, and then organized delivery by airdrops or by boat, or sometimes by submarine. I longed to meet some of these agents, and later on, I did. I not only met them, but worked with some of them.

Another committee was the Administration of Territories (Europe) Committee. It dealt with planning for the administration of territories as they were liberated by Allied forces. The committee had to plan with a great many unknowns, and prepare for various contingencies. The aim was to move in as an area was liberated and assist the local people to re-establish control as quickly as possible. The work on this committee helped to prepare me for my later work in the Foreign Office, which focused on similar problems in post-war Germany.

Sometimes you would get a glimpse into other activities. One young Colonel who was a member of the ACS had a secretariat task of which he never spoke. He had a special connection with Professor Charles Ellis, the War Office Scientific Advisor, a mystery figure about whom the rest of us knew nothing. One day I overheard a cryptic conversation between this Colonel and the Brigadier, which I did not understand at the time. Much later, I realised that they were referring to the atomic bomb project and to the Anglo–American Quebec Agreement of 1943 about the participation of British scientists in the Manhattan Project.

All through the War I sat on the second floor of one of the pepper pot towers of the War Office. There were three desks in this big room, and mine was in the window embrasure, and very exposed. The War Office itself was built of massive masonry as if modelled on the Tower of London, so when we heard the siren, we sheltered in the heavy stone arches on the landing until the All Clear was sounded. After our windows were blown in for the second time, the glass was replaced with scrim.

During the War, there were small oases of beauty. The famous pianist, Myra Hess, organized daily lunch time concerts in the National Gallery, after its art treasures had been packed up and sent for safety to caves in the Welsh mountains. We would go and listen to various well known artists, often in Service uniforms. I particularly remember pianists and string quartets. An enterprising society lady, known to us all as Poppy, gathered volunteers and set up a stall supplying coffee and sandwiches to us concert goers. How did she manage to organize the supplies in those days of shortage? We never knew. I also bought a subscription to *Artists of Fame and Promise* at a small art gallery, and called in whenever I had a few moments to spare.

As D-Day drew nearer, the pace of work in the War Office, and in the ACS, accelerated. We were working flat out, with very long hours, and it was a stressful time. I was exhausted – we all were – and I had a painful back. My doctor urged me to take a week's sick leave. Next morning, when I reached the office Alan pre-empted me. Before I could say a word, he told me that he had been ordered to take a fortnight's complete rest. He asked if I could hold the fort in his absence. What could I say but 'Yes'?

I returned to my doctor and explained the situation. Somewhat reluctantly she gave me two prescriptions, one for Benzedrine, a stimulant, and one for some powerful sleeping tablets. Benzedrine was a new drug which was given to fighter pilots. It was not normally prescribed to civilians.

What an exhilarating experience! Benzedrine made everything so easy and nothing was a problem. I got through a tremendous amount of work. I wrote at great speed without hesitation or uncertainty. The shorthand typists begged me not to dictate so fast. It was effortless, but I had an uneasy feeling that this might all be an illusion, and that I might simply be writing nonsense, because my critical faculties had ceased to function. Luckily, there was no thunderbolt from the Brigadier.

Then I had a summons from the Permanent Secretary of the War Office. Sir Frederick Bovenschen, Sir James Grigg's successor. I was sure I must have done something monumentally dreadful to be called to his presence. I pictured him reading a paper I had written and thinking, 'Why did this woman write *Jabberwocky* over and over again?', but I felt quite light-hearted as I walked to his office. 'Bovers', a small elderly man wearing a pince-nez, greeted me kindly. He wanted to discuss a committee paper I had written on a subject of particular interest to him. He asked a few detailed questions, which I answered to his satisfaction. As I left, I was relieved to know I had not been writing nonsense after all!

I held the fort for two weeks, and then went back to the doctor, who was surprised to see me still on my feet. She gave me a certificate for a short rest, barely more than a week. I went off to stay in a lovely cottage in the country, near my old home in Surrey. D-Day, that long-awaited date, came while I was there recuperating. Thousands of lorries and tanks had been parked in the thick woods running down the southern slopes of the Hog's Back. From the little cottage on the hillside, I heard the tremendous roar as they left their hiding places and trundled down to the coast. It was hugely exciting to hear this great army on the move, on its way to invade Europe.

Shortly after D-Day, Bovers summoned me and told me that he had already turned down several requests to transfer me to other departments. Now the Foreign Office had asked for me. It meant a promotion. What did I wish to do? I said, 'I should hate to leave the War Office, but it does sound interesting, and I can't say no.' And so I was transferred to the Foreign Office, to work on the planning for the occupation of Germany when the War was over.

My new office was at Norfolk House, in St. James's Square. There was a small staff of around a dozen under Sir Ivone Kirkpatrick and the somewhat eccentric General S. W. Kirby, who was a brilliant military engineer with strange passion for the Lost Tribes of Israel and the secrets of the Pyramids. Although I did not speak German and had no specialist knowledge, they recruited me because of my useful secretariat experience. I was to head a section of the Secretariat. I had three majors on my staff, and my grade was that of Principal. It was an unusual role for a woman.

We spent the last months of 1944 planning for transport, food supplies, and trade, as well as the reconstruction of the German health and education systems. As the invasion proceeded, policies for the occupation of Germany were being developed at the highest level by the Foreign Secretaries of the Western Allies, and all work was governed by their decisions. Various experts were called in to advise: Sir Robert Birley, headmaster of Charterhouse and later Eton, helped us with education, while Professor Alec Cairncross and Ernst Schumacher advised on economic questions. Schumacher had worked with Lord Beveridge on the post-war plans for the Welfare State, and later wrote two popular and highly influential books: *Small is Beautiful* and *A Guide for the Perplexed*. We recruited a small pool of interpreters – at first little more than a puddle – who began practising in mock committee meetings. The unit also came to incorporate some senior civil servants, experts in topics such as food supply, electricity, transport, and civil engineering.

The staff was very mixed. Besides this solid core, there were a few mavericks, including a defrocked Russian Orthodox priest, and Colonel Wintle, a daredevil adventurer who had become famous for flying a single-seater aircraft up the Thames under the bridges for a bet.

Three people whom I came to know well came from the Intelligence Corps. They were young officers: two English and one Canadian, all Russian-speakers, who had been leading lives of high adventure in the mountains of Yugoslavia. There was Nicky van der Vliet from a Scottish Canadian regiment, who always wore a kilt. Although his name was Dutch, he was Russian by birth; his family had settled in Russia in the time of Peter the Great, but had fled to Canada during the Russian Revolution. Then there was Jasper Rootham, the son of an English Professor of Music. He wrote a good book later about the war in the Balkans, called *Miss Fire*. When I arrived at Norfolk House he greeted me with the words: 'Thank God you've come! Now I can take a week's leave and get married to my lovely ballet dancer!' The third was an aristocratic Scotsman called Rupert Raw. I remember him telling me about their first airdrop into a dark forest in Yugoslavia. They fortified themselves with a stiff drink for the drop, and fell singing into the top of a tree. They deplored the change when the Allies decided to back the Yugoslavian resistance leaders Tito and Mihailović was abandoned. When they were sent back jobless to England, they were quickly seconded to the Foreign Office.

My number two was a brilliant young star of the literary firmament, reputed to be intimate with Elizabeth Bowen and Rosamond Lehmann – his name was Goronwy Rees. The son of a Welsh nonconformist minister, he got a scholarship to Oxford, and had been a young Fellow of All Souls, proud of his Brythonic[3] background. Before the War he had written for the *Spectator*, and he always secretly enjoyed the idea of an obscure boy from Wales mixing with the fashionable literati.

When he was an undergraduate in Oxford he was asked by some young aristocrat, 'Oh, I see you are from Wales. Do you know the Angleseys?'

'I only know one', he replied, 'and I call it Ynys Môn.' [4]

It seemed absurd for me to be senior to such a well-known figure. Goronwy often lunched at the Ritz with his glamorous friends, so I always made a point of being on hand to stand in for him at afternoon meetings if necessary.

He had an intimate knowledge of Germany and German intellectual life. He had spent much time in Germany (as had Spender, Auden, and Isherwood), and he knew his way around the rather louche underground of pre-war Berlin. Goronwy came with us to Germany in 1945 as a member of the Control Commission Political Division, where his experience and German contacts must have been invaluable. I lost touch with him after leaving Berlin. Years later it emerged that, as a good writer with left-wing sympathies and literary contacts, he had been the kind of 'sleeping agent' the Soviets used to recruit. He became Principal of the University College of Wales Aberystwyth, but was outed for his Communist past and had to retire early. Years later, after his death, his daughter Jenny wrote a book about his life, called *Looking for Mr. Nobody*.

Looking back, I admire the way the planning for the occupation of Germany went ahead. The plans had to take account of all the three powers, Britain, the US, and Russia. The details were negotiated in the European Advisory Commission, which had senior representatives

---

[3] An authentic primeval Celt
[4] Welsh name for the Isle of Anglesey

from the three powers. The process was complicated by the fact that the Allies were so different. Churchill was frustrated and disappointed by Roosevelt's willingness to defer to Stalin. He called Britain 'the little donkey caught between the Russian Bear and the American Buffalo', although he added that 'the little donkey knows its way home.' In 1945 France joined the post-war group of Allies, and so from that point forward all plans for post-war occupation involved the four powers: Britain, the US, Russia, and France.

The European Advisory Commission came up with a scheme in which each Ally would be responsible for its own zone, a portion of Germany, which it would administer independently within the four-power framework. Berlin was to be the occupation capital, and would also be divided into four sectors. There would be a council, the Allied Control Council, which would coordinate administration of Germany. Each Ally would be responsible for the cost of administering its own zone, which would prove to be a huge burden.

When the papers came through to us in Norfolk House, I remember seeing the map defining the four zones and the four sectors of Berlin, which was to be the centre of government, and in which each nation would have its own separate area. I was horrified to see the British Allied Control staff in Berlin would be miles from the British Zone, and the lines of communication would run through the Russian Zone and be very vulnerable. If there was any trouble they could easily be cut. So I rushed off to see Sir Ivone Kirkpatrick, and voice my concerns. 'Sir this is intolerable! It must be altered! Look at our lines of communication. Suppose the Russians decide to cut us off, we would be helpless!' There was never trust between the Allies. He just said 'This has been settled at the highest level. Stop worrying and go back to work.'

I am sure he was at least as concerned as I was, but there was nothing he could do. The danger was all too clear, as we saw later when Russia blockaded West Berlin, and the huge Berlin Airlift became necessary.

When VE Day came on May 8, 1945, it was just a date in the calendar to me. I was so weary that although I was hugely relieved, I did not go out into the streets to join in the public celebrations. Nevertheless, VE Day signalled a transition. Our group had always known that when Germany surrendered, it would be time for us to begin executing the plans we had been creating. Soon, we would be heading to Berlin.

Chapter 7

Berlin

Once hostilities had come to an end and the Act of Surrender had been signed, our small advance guard departed for Germany to start setting up the Control Commission office. It was June 1945. Shortly before we were due to leave, a journalist friend rang me to suggest a lunch date. None of the dates he suggested were possible for me, because we would have left for Germany by then, but as this was still a secret, I simply told him I was too busy and gave him no further information. Nevertheless he managed to put two and two together, and the presumed date for our departure was published in the *Observer*.

We flew out in a military Dakota transport. There were no luxuries like seats – you just sat on your suitcase on the floor, surrounded by luggage. About a score of us, mainly female and mainly civilian, were packed into the aircraft and flown to a small landing strip in the British Zone. Our destination was just a muddy field and a small wooden hut, with an NCO brewing up a cup of tea. I was the most senior, so when we arrived the other women asked me, 'Please Miss Rainbow, where's the Ladies?' I marched into the hut and enquired after the facilities.

'Well, there's an 'ole in the 'edge', was the stolid reply.

One by one the ladies took his kindly advice and tiptoed through the mud into the neighbouring field.

We were then packed into lorries and driven to a little Westphalian market town called Bad Oeynhausen, where we stayed while awaiting further orders. The town was undamaged by the War, rustic and verdant, and I was impressed by the high standard of German working class housing, with its double-glazing and efficient coke stoves. From here, there was no sense of the devastation that existed in other parts of Germany.

Bad Oeynhausen was the temporary administrative headquarters for the British zone. On one memorable occasion, General

Montgomery, whose own headquarters were nearby at Celle, came to inspect us. German civilians were ordered indoors and motorcycles patrolled the streets while the General was there. We lined up, and he walked down the lines, exchanging a word with each one of us. He came to my friend Kay, a senior commander in the Auxiliary Territorial Service (ATS).

'And what did you do in civilian life before the War?' he asked kindly.

She saluted smartly. 'Sir, I was Deputy Procurator Fiscal for Argyll and the Western Isles,' she replied. This was an impressive position for a young woman in those days, and the answer clearly surprised the great general. He was lost for words.

Before long, orders came. I was to go to Berlin with my friends Sally and Kay to set up the Berlin offices for the Control Commission. The drive up to Berlin was terrific. We travelled in a splendid big Opel with an army driver. It was an all-day drive, about 300 miles. We drove the whole way on an autobahn, a type of road then unknown outside Germany. We did not pass through a single town for the entire journey – there was nothing like this in England. Nor did we see signs of damage from the war. Much of the way was through forests, with stopping places at intervals with outdoor tables. All the traffic was military: tanks and army lorries. There was nothing else.

The first sign of life on the outskirts of Berlin was a Russian checkpoint, and my anxieties about the Russian control of our supply lines were reawakened. We could see they had chosen particularly primitive and ferocious types to man the checkpoints; there was an air of menace. The Russian soldiers were wearing looted watches all the way up their arms. Why so many? It seems that watches were a novelty to them, and they did not understand that they needed winding up; when they ran down, they would just help themselves to more. We three girls, with our one soldier driver, felt very uneasy, but eventually they waved us through.

We arrived in Berlin in the evening. It was cold and drizzling and we could not believe what we saw. We drove through streets of just rubble and ruin, with nobody much in sight at all and hardly a house standing. It was an extraordinary, unbelievable sight to see a big city that was ruined as far as you could see. We drove in the rain through

Berlin, 1945
Brandenburg Gate

endless streets of completely demolished buildings, and as dusk was falling we finally reached the British HQ. It was a shock after being in Germany for several weeks, where we had seen nothing that showed us the devastation of the war. I had seen the destruction in London from bombing, but this was incomparably worse.

We spoke to the NCO at HQ. He gave our driver the address of our billet and gave us our supplies: a roll of bedding each, a huge box of Camel cigarettes, a jerry can of water, and a quantity of cheap German gin. 'For Heaven's sake,' the NCO said, 'don't drink the tap water.' Then we were driven off to our temporary billet, three one-bedroom flats on the three floors of a small block that was rather battered, but empty at least and, compared to most of Berlin, relatively undamaged.

I got the ground floor flat, which was just a bedroom, sitting room, and kitchen. The others had the two flats above. Many of the windows were broken. There was some very basic furniture: an iron Army bedstead to spread out your bedroll, a table, and a chair – that was about it. Each flat had a small kitchen with a gas cooker, a table, and a sink. The gas stove produced such a tiny bead of flame that it was not really usable; it would take an hour to heat a kettle of water. If you turned on the tap, the water trickled out, but you could not it use it because it was very badly polluted. It must have been dreadful trying to get the water supply going again, because there were so many corpses in underground tunnels where people had sheltered. There was this sickly smell everywhere: the smell of unburied bodies, some underground and even some just left out in the open.

We went to bed early in our separate flats, and in the night I could hear Russian soldiers in the street outside. They had not yet been pulled back into the Russian Zone of Berlin, and they were all over the city, roaring up and down the streets, shouting drunken songs, and firing into the air. Looting was common. There were bullet marks all over the outside of the building, and as I was on the ground floor, I thought, 'What do I do if someone comes through the window?' We felt completely unprotected.

In the morning an Army car came to take us to the office. It was just a big empty office building, stacked with packing cases, which we were to set in order. The occupying army was already there in Berlin, and more or less in control of the city, but the government in the form of the Allied Control Council still had to be installed. The first day we spent making new friends, meeting old ones, and exchanging news. I told a naval officer about our anxious night, and he said, 'I'll lend you my spare revolver.'

I had learned at the rifle range under the War Office, but I had never used a revolver. He showed me how to fire it, saying, 'For God's sake, if you see anybody at the window, or you're threatened in any way, don't aim at them — just fire, and hope it will frighten them away.'

I slept with the revolver under my pillow for a while, until the Russian troops were withdrawn to their own sector, and the early lawlessness settled down. Luckily, I never needed to use it.

Settling in was very peculiar. Fairly soon, Kay moved off to ATS quarters, and a civilian friend and I got a beautiful little furnished flat on the Grunewald, a park-like residential area of Berlin which was largely undamaged. We had a young German maid, Hilde, to do the housework. She was sweet, and always singing folksongs. One day, out of the blue, an elderly German gentleman called at the flat to see how his old home had fared. He was concerned for his books and his piano, and obviously feared the worst; he must have been relieved to find that

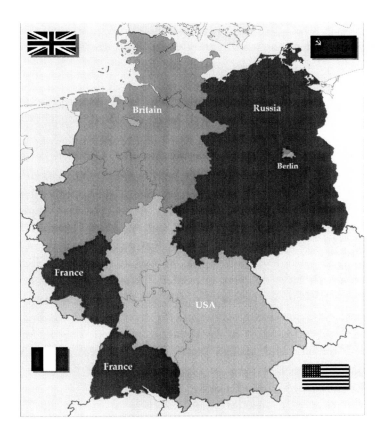

Zones of Allied Control after WWII

two English ladies were in residence, rather than the rude soldiery he had feared.

We got on with setting up the Control Commission office from scratch. It was located in a utilitarian concrete office block, near the Brandenburg Gate, selected for its location and because it had not been destroyed. One of the first tasks was to load the papers that we had brought with us into filing cabinets, but there were no filing cabinets in this big office block. We eventually acquired some, loaded up the files and got to work. People were turning up all the time, meeting each other, and sorting things out. The offices were swept and cleaned by German cleaning women, whom we never saw, and often they would leave a bunch of wild flowers in a glass jar on my desk. It was a small but homely touch. In this utter desolation, wild flowers springing everywhere out of the ruins were a consolation. In the streets, where there were no shops, you would see little roadside kiosks selling bunches of flowers.

The system of committees that had been responsible for the planning of the occupation had been dissolved when Germany surrendered. I was now working in an organization with the rather unwieldy name of Control Commission for Germany – British Element. This body was responsible for the day-to-day administration of the British Zone of occupied Germany, and coordinating its activities with local groups, the British Army, the Government in London, especially the Foreign Office, and the Allied Control Council. I was in the Central Secretariat, a team that included experts in topics such as economics and food supply, as well as generalists who could take on a wide range of tasks as needed. Though we had done much contingency planning before the fall of Germany we could not anticipate every possible situation, so the working methods had to be able to respond to events as the situation unfolded. The organization included military and civilian staff. As a Principal my rank was considered to be equivalent to Lieutenant Colonel: the army clerks would address me as 'Miss Rainbow, Sir!'

Our first task was to establish communications with Zone Headquarters and government departments in London. Next, we had to organize our work under the four-power government of the whole of Germany by the Allied Control Council, generally known as the Kommandatura, which consisted of the four commanders-in-chief and their staffs.

Each occupying power in Germany was responsible within its own zone, but policy for the whole country had to be coordinated, and this was the responsibility of the Allied Control Council. It involved much international discussion, and often disagreement. Although much of our work took place in our own British Element offices, we spent a great deal of time in the Allied Control Council building with our colleagues from the other nations. It could have been a very unwieldy arrangement, but it worked surprisingly smoothly, all things considered, because at the very apex there were the four commanders-in-chief.

There was the great Russian General George Zhukov, who was a tremendous personality. When he came into the Council room, you were immediately aware of him. You did not have to speak Russian; you just knew that here was a big, big man. Zhukov had an enthusiastic woman interpreter in army uniform. When he spoke in meetings, she would listen to him with rapt attention, then, slapping her thigh and laughing, she would announce 'My general, he say…'

There was our very excellent General Brian Robertson, who had a modest yet commanding presence, and then General Lucius Clay from the US, and the French General Koenig. They made up the leadership of the Council. Under them were their deputies, and under the deputies were Directorates, each of which had representatives from each of the four powers. Each Directorate was responsible for all the big policy issues within a particular area, such as politics, military affairs, economics, health, and so on.

There were very different attitudes among the four occupying powers taking part in the discussions. The Americans were volatile: at first they had proposed the very harsh Morgenthau plan, which would have de-industrialized Germany and reduced it to a country of subsistence farmers, but they were now generous in their food and other supply programmes. The Economic Directorate had set the agreed minimum rations for the German population at 1200 calories a day, which was very low, just enough to survive, and the Americans tried to increase this to 3000 calories. I remember very well a meeting at which this was discussed among the Directorate, and the Americans were appalled at the thought of people living on 1200 calories a day. The Russians had no sympathy for people who were suffering on 1200 calories a day, as their country was on the verge of mass starvation, and the British and French had little sympathy, as both countries were on meagre rations. Rationing was actually more severe in Britain *after* the War than it had been during the War because Britain was diverting food to Northern Europe. In part this was for relief aid to the Dutch, who were in desperate straits, but it was also to keep our zone in Germany from starvation. This caused the three powers of Britain, Russia, and France to join forces and say, 'We are not going to have the Germans fed better than our people at home!'

There was also friction amongst the powers in the Allied Control Council over reparations, and the removal of German industrial plant by the Russians. The joke went round that the Russians would take away a hole in the ground if they could transport it profitably.

Another great point of contention and uncertainty was the extent to which 'de-Nazification' should be attempted. To remove all members of the Nazi party from official positions would inevitably cause the collapse of existing administrative structures, and would be unrealistic since every incumbent German official was bound to be at least outwardly a Nazi, however inwardly reluctant. Nor were there enough Allied resources to replace everyone who had Nazi affiliations at the most local levels of government. Then there was the problem of how to deal with the German armed forces, where a sudden demobilization would have let loose a flood of unemployed, unpaid and disorganized fighting men. One also had to take account of the very strong bonds formed by men who have fought together. These issues had been the subjects of much careful thought in advance of the occupation, but now it was a matter of dealing with the actual problems on the ground, in agreement with the four Allies. The care taken in the planning of the occupation brought remarkable success in post-war Germany, and should have provided useful lessons for later politicians.

At first I did rather general work. I was asked to compile a review of the state of Germany for the first six months of the occupation, with regard to food, transport, health, and so on. My report caught the eye of Sir Percy Mills of the Economic Directorate, and he asked to have me transferred onto his staff. I demurred, saying that I had no knowledge of economics, but he brushed aside this objection: 'I don't care, I can understand what you write.' I quickly found myself a member of the Economic Directorate, which would have interesting consequences for me.

Under the Economic Directorate, which consisted of the four national representatives, there were several subsidiary four-power bodies that dealt with food supplies, transport, industry and labour, and so on. The Economic Directorate itself met in the same fine building as the Allied Control Council itself, its entrance guarded by white-gloved American soldiers. The Economic Directorate gathered once or twice a week, in meetings which often lasted a full day from ten o'clock until as late as eight o'clock in the evening. There was a great deal to discuss, with issues which were often complex and technical coming down from

Allied Control Council building, Berlin

our masters, the four commanders-in-chief, and up from the specialist sub-directorates.

In between meetings, the Secretariat had to circulate papers in three languages (English, French, and Russian), prepare agenda papers, agree upon translations, write minutes of the meetings, and follow through on previous decisions. It was hard work because of intrinsic difficulties and conflicting national attitudes, and sometimes misunderstandings arose due to problems in the translations. The four Allied nations took turns in providing the Chairman and two Secretaries for a month at a time. In theory, the participants spoke their own language with an interpreter. The French were very accommodating, in that all spoke English and some spoke Russian.

The Duty Secretaries did the minutes in their own languages, and then they would go to the interpreters and the translation would be agreed to. It made for very hard work and naturally took quite a time when you had interpreters in the meetings. It was a far cry from the brilliant simultaneous translation facilities available at my last big international conference, in Vienna in 1999. The difficulties of this way of working drew the Secretariats closer together, and the working relationship between the four Secretaries in the Economic Directorate was very good. We got on well, and I never saw any friction. Our relations with the Americans and French were close, but we also enjoyed a good relationship with our Russian colleagues, in spite of language difficulties.

The job of Secretary was truly demanding. The Americans had several Secretaries, and the Russians a couple, but I did the job alone, until a young major was sent to help me. At one meeting, he was asked by one of the Russians,

'As a man, don't you object to working under a woman?'

'Not at all,' replied my major. 'Lorna has the most experience to do the job.'

'No Russian man would put up with that!' responded our Russian colleague.

'I thought Russia was the home of equality between the sexes,' I said, and a young woman on the Russian staff spoke up.

'Oh yes,' she said. 'We can work just as hard as the men, share the danger, and do all the heavy labour that they do, but we don't get the good jobs.'

Our social intercourse with the Russians was more restricted. We were on the best of terms inside the office, but we were less successful when we tried to make dates to meet them outside. They were not allowed to fraternize. I did have two good friends among the Russian staff, however. The first was an elderly lawyer, old-fashioned and courteous, who spoke good French, so we were able to communicate directly. He left Berlin quite soon, and was replaced by a young Red Army major who had been wounded on the Eastern Front. Volodya spoke fluent English with a strong Brooklyn accent, because his father had been a Soviet trade attaché in the United States when he was a child.

On one occasion when I had to return to London for several days of meetings at the Foreign Office, Volodya asked if I would get something for him. He wanted a copy of *Alice in Wonderland*, with the Tenniel illustrations. He had had one as a little boy, but it was lost. When I reached London, I went to Foyles and found a copy. He was absolutely delighted.

Work in Berlin was intensely interesting and filled up most of one's waking hours, but outside work I found life in the city almost unbearably depressing. The sight of so much appalling destruction, and the evidence of human suffering on such a scale were often intolerable.

Debris was still being removed by hand by gangs of women with buckets; no rebuilding had started as yet. In that pre-television age, one was unprepared for images of such desolation. It inspired constant feelings of horror. The haggard survivors looked like zombies, very white and dazed. They wandered around, hardly troubling to move out of the way of traffic. They did not seem to know where they were. In those early days there was no way to convey to the outside world what it was like. No wonder Churchill wept when he saw Berlin in 1945. I never got hardened to it. I felt I was living in the *City of Dreadful Night*.

> *O melancholy Brothers, dark, dark, dark!*
> *O battling in black floods without an ark!*
> *O spectral wanderers of unholy Night!*
> *My soul hath bled for you these sunless years,*
> *With bitter blood-drops running down like tears:*
> *Oh dark, dark, dark, withdrawn from joy and light!*

- James "B.V." Thomson

The first winter in Berlin was intensely cold, and in the British sector we were very short of food, though we were vastly better off than German civilians. In Berlin, our staff ate the same Spartan rations as those at home in Britain. Some of our messes were in old buildings which were bomb damaged, and the snow used to come in under the door and around the windows; we were very short of fuel. It was so cold that we used sit down in our messes for lunch with our sheepskin coats and gloves on, taking our gloves off to eat and putting them on again immediately. We seemed to live on mashed potatoes, soya link sausages, and Spam, and we were cold all the time. That winter it was so cold that the lake near where we were living was frozen so deep that the Army drove ten-ton trunks across it for a short cut, rather than going round.

Occasionally friends from the US sector would invite us to go over to one of the American messes, which were very well heated. There was what was seemed an almost indecent amount of food and drink in the American messes, and the attitudes were as different as our rations. I was shocked to see some of the Americans drop cigarette ash into the food left on their plates. Were they unaware that the leftovers would be taken by the waiters to feed their families?

The monthly rotation of the chair of the Directorate meetings included responsibility for providing a buffet lunch in an adjoining room. Each nation followed a different policy. British lunches were somewhat frugal. American lunches were ample, consisting largely of hamburgers and other American specialties. French lunches were elegantly presented, with good wines, but not extravagant. Russian lunches were lavish to the point of ostentation, with caviar, exotic fruits, Russian champagne, and vodka.

One of the Brits, a major who came to meetings sometimes, was intrigued by the pink champagne of the Russian lunches. 'Pink champagne, pink champagne,' he mused. 'I want blue champagne!' Not long afterwards I hosted a small party, and I doctored a bottle of white wine with just a few harmless drops of Royal Blue Quink (a brand of ink) and handed him a glass, saying 'Blue champagne, blue champagne.'

For us civilian women, life had an extraordinary unreality. We were all individuals uprooted and forming an artificial society, without families, children, community organizations, or any social arrangements beyond messes and nightclubs. Even if one had wanted to take the air among the rubble, it was not safe to go out for a walk. It took time for law and order to be re-established, and I would very quickly have lost my handbag with all my vital documents in it, if nothing else. This was the lawless world seen in the spy novels of Len Deighton or John LeCarré. It was the sheer lack of community that I found so depressing. No shopping to do, no library to go to, no cafes to meet in, nowhere to get your hair cut.

The only social structures were the officers' clubs. It was in one of these, in August 1945, that we chanced to hear on the wireless a brief announcement of the bombing of Hiroshima. What struck me was the strength of the officers' reactions. These men had seen all-out war as they fought their way across Europe, and they were at that very moment in a bomb-devastated city. The news came over the radio, and we listened, and we could not believe it. One Army officer – not a softie, a tough soldier – said 'My God, that's not the way to fight a war. *That* is wrong!' There was a feeling that this was beyond the rules of war, a feeling of great shock.

Just once I got out of Berlin into the countryside. My maverick naval friend, the one who had lent me the revolver in my hour of need, liberated a jeep and we made a break for it. We came across a large building standing alone in open heathland and went in. It was an isolation hospital, full of sick children, refugees from eastern Germany who had lost their parents. There were two nurses there, but no guards. The nurses offered to show us round, and we found dozens of ill children, emaciated and covered in sores. Even so, some were standing up in their cots and throwing pillows at each other, irrepressibly playing in spite of everything. We went to see their lunch being cooked, a watery soup of potatoes and onions in a huge iron cauldron. We had quite a collection of ration chocolate in the back of the car, and we left it for them, though it could not have gone far among so many.

A French colleague offered me the opportunity to escape from the relentless gloom of Berlin. She asked if I would like to visit her parents in Paris, who would, she was sure, welcome me as a guest. Indeed they did; they lived in a beautiful apartment in Neuilly, and although at that time rations were very restricted in Paris, they had ample supplies from the farm they owned in Normandy. I was glad to be able to take them some real coffee from the American PX in Berlin, a welcome change from their usual brew of dandelion roots and acorns. They left me very much to my own devices, but kept me well supplied with information and books about Paris and France. I explored the city, alone and on foot, for a week, and had a wonderful break. I enjoyed a visit to the old artists' quarters in Montmartre, where I called on an elderly artist, a friend of one of my American colleagues, in her ramshackle studio-cum-apartment. I went to High Mass at Notre Dame, and received an unexpected blessing from the Archbishop of Paris as he passed down the aisles.

Back in Berlin, life continued its unreal course between the long office hours and the relentless round of dancing and drinking in the clubs and bars. This might have been fun for a time, but it soon palled. The highlight of my time there, the thing I remember with joy, was going to the State Opera. Two British officers, who were passionate music-lovers, had discovered that the Berlin Staatsoper in the Russian sector was up and running, though in a rather battered state. They took me along with them. Going into the Russian sector was a great adventure in itself at that time. We walked to it through the ruinous tunnels of the underground railway, and as we approached the opera house we saw elderly Germans, formally attired in evening dress, gallantly making their way through the rubble. We saw an excellent production of *Eugene Onegin* with tremendous singers: Tiana Lemnitz, a great dramatic soprano, and Willi Dongraf-Fassbender, the famous bass. It was a wonderful evening, and a great performance by any standards.

My friends and I went to the State Opera several times. Gluck's *Orfeo and Euridice* was popular, but more often than not we would go expecting Mozart and find a notice when we got there saying that 'by popular request' it was an altogether different opera, one beloved of the Russians, most often *Eugene Onegin*. We were fortunate to hear, in these battered surroundings, world-class singers at the height of their powers. I especially remember the exquisite young coloratura soprano, Erna Berger.

I visited the Russian Orthodox Church at Easter for Midnight Mass. It was a modest, round building without seats or pews. You sat or stood on the bare floor, while the old and infirm sat on stone benches around the walls. I loved the music, from a small group of half a dozen men and women in drab raincoats who sang so beautifully. When the time for the sermon came, the Archimandrite, a dignified old man with a white beard and a serene and kindly face, came and sat on a chair in front of the screen. The children flocked to sit at his feet. Although I could not understand a word, I was moved to see this venerable figure surrounded by attentive children. I was also impressed by the presence of several Red Army soldiers.

By the autumn of 1946, it had become clear that some new way of financing the British Zone would have to be found. It was the most highly industrialized, the most severely damaged, and the most heavily populated, and therefore the most expensive for the occupying power. Relief and reconstruction were a huge burden, and Britain, already virtually bankrupted by the War, could not sustain it. The British government decided to seek some agreement with the Americans which would spread the costs more evenly. In this connection, I went to London to do some work at the Foreign Office.

While I was there, Sir Mark Turner, an old Whitehall friend, bounded into my office and told me that a delegation was shortly to go to the US to discuss possible adjustments to the costs of our two zones. I was to be included. I asked 'For how long? Is it all right with Berlin?'

'Oh, I should think three weeks,' he replied. 'General Robertson agrees.' Suddenly, I found myself preparing to go to Washington.

Chapter 8

Washington

I joined the British delegation which was to be sent to Washington to propose that, while the two nations should continue to administer their separate zones, the unequal costs should be redistributed on a fifty–fifty basis. The delegation included Commander-in-Chief General Robertson with Sir William Strang, Sir David Waley, and other Whitehall notables.

I went to London for preparatory meetings, and then the party sailed for New York on the Queen Mary, a luxury liner recently restored after war duty as a troop ship. The voyage, though luxurious, was packed with hard work, as briefings and meetings were held every day on board. We commoners had special passes from Cabin Class to attend briefings with the top brass in First Class. Once, I turned a corner in the company of the former British Consul, Michael Robb, in New York, and came face to face with the Duke and Duchess of Windsor. 'Michael Robb!' she exclaimed. 'What are you doing here?' I was struck by her white face and black hair, and by her skeletal thinness. As for the Duke, I had a sudden flashback to the British Empire exhibition at Wembley in 1926, where I had seen a life-sized statue of the Prince of Wales sculpted in golden New Zealand butter. How disappointing to see him in the flesh, twenty years later.

We came into New York in November of 1946, on a wintery-feeling evening. The city looked quite magical in the twilight, with little pinpricks of light flickering into life. Our huge ship moved slowly into the harbour, and by the time it had touched with exquisite precision against the pier, millions of tiny lights were shining softly all around. It was enchanting!

The British team took the train to Washington, and work began there next day. We had three weeks of hard discussion with the American representatives, who were keen to minimize additional costs to their country, while we were naturally aiming for the greatest possible relief. I was very fortunate to be present in the meetings and thoroughly involved, not simply working in the back room as I had expected. I found this first-hand experience of international discussions most illuminating. It gave me some insights which were unexpectedly useful to me much later in my working life. After three weeks of hard work and strongly contested debate, the effective team effort on the British side produced the result we had hoped for: a fifty–fifty division of costs. The resulting two-zone structure was commonly known as 'Bizonia'. The British Foreign Secretary, Ernest Bevin, came out to Washington to sign the agreement.

At the end of the mission there was a splendid celebratory dinner at the Mayflower Hotel. I sat next to Sir Mark Turner, who remarked to me that the agreement would mean extra work for the British Embassy staff in Washington, and that the Foreign Office would have to send reinforcements. A posting to Washington was much sought after, so I was surprised and delighted when Mark told me I had been chosen to go. It was likely that the work would require two people at the Embassy, and I should probably be joined very shortly by a colleague, though this had not yet been decided. I would be able to spend Christmas at home with my family before starting in Washington in the New Year.

At the end of negotiations, most of the delegation returned to England. Dougal Malcolm and I were left with the tedious task of clearing up: paying bills, destroying documents that should not be retained, and writing the many thank-you notes to all of the parties involved. Just before we left, we received a charming invitation from a senior diplomat at the Embassy, Sir Roger Makins, later Lord Sherfield, to join him and his wife, Lady Alice, for dinner. Sir Roger looked the part of an authoritative and aristocratic leader, with a tall, slim figure, an aquiline profile and a strong presence. I was to encounter him again, many years later, when he was the head of the Atomic Energy Authority, and again when, as a Fellow of All Souls in Oxford, he would invite me to dinner there from time to time.

I returned to Berlin to clear my desk and say goodbye. One of the more affecting goodbyes was with Hilde, our German maid, who burst into tears and begged me to stay. I was sad to leave her.

After spending Christmas in London with my family, I flew to New York in January 1947 to begin my new job. At that time, flights to the United States were few and far between, and I believe they were only available for official travel. There were few civilian airliners, and the new London airport at Heathrow consisted of an open field and a few hangars. Several times (three, if I remember rightly) I went to the air terminal in Kensington only to be told that no aircraft was available, and to come back on another day. But eventually I was off! The flight, in a propeller aircraft, took about 15 hours, with a fuelling stopover in Newfoundland. Gander Airport was a wilderness of snow, with one or two hangars and some stalls selling Eskimo artefacts to shivering travellers waiting for their connecting flights. At the time, no one had any conception of what air travel would become.

Lodgings had been found for me in a large apartment overlooking Rock Creek Park in Washington. As well as my landlady, there were two other lodgers, both American girls working in US government departments. One came from Alabama and one from New England, and any simple ideas I may have held of the 'American accent' were quickly dispelled. My neighbour from Alabama spoke in plangent tones that sounded like a lament to my ears, and at first I thought she was in distress. Washington, I later realized, was a melting pot for people from all over the United States, so that one found a wide diversity of accents and manners there. From my lodgings it was just a short walk to the British Embassy, where my new job began the next day.

My new city seemed very open and friendly, and much of the old frontier spirit of ready hospitality still prevailed. At first I found it heart-warming, but in time I realized that this easy familiarity was not necessarily more kindly than English reserve. I encountered various reactions to me as a new arrival. Some people whom I met were fulsome in their admiration for 'your brave little country', while some others thought little of Britain's contribution to winning the war. Yet others were shocked by the post-war election which had replaced the Prime Minister Winston Churchill with the Labour Party's Clement Attlee. Britain, one man told me, was going to hell in a handcart under 'that Red'. Such misunderstandings were mutual. When I spoke admiringly of the great President Roosevelt, I was surprised to find that

Lorna in Washington, DC

my feelings were by no means universally shared in his own country. There were more surprises to come.

Since the new agreement required Britain to pay half the cost of the British and American Zones, it was necessary to keep a running account of the respective contributions. We had to monitor the programme of procurement and shipping in order to secure the best possible conditions for Britain – for instance, by using British shipping and sterling sources of supply wherever possible. The Cunard office acted as our shipping agents, and I was always on the alert for shipping that was ready to leave US ports for Germany. Whenever an opportunity arose, I was quick to let Cunard know.

Information poured into our office from Germany and London, including detailed lists of requirements for food and other supplies. We tracked all British procurement and shipments, including the costs of handling, freight and insurance. All the British figures were in pounds, shillings and pence, and long tons, while the American information was in dollars and short tons, which meant that there was a great deal of conversion to do before one could make comparisons. To make matters worse, all the British procurement was done in London, albeit in consultation with the Washington end. There were no computers or calculators to help me; I had no aids beyond my own brain. Eventually someone produced a comptometer, a mechanical calculating device produced by the British Tabulating Machine Company, to assist my work. It all seems very remote and primitive now.

The balance was struck at the end of every quarter. If the British contribution was less than fifty percent, the Embassy would have to send a large dollar cheque to the US Government. I personally carried some horrendously large cheques across Washington. Although the most interesting work was watching out for the shipping opportunities, what kept me at my desk at night were the computations.

I now had a colleague, Lieutenant-Colonel Peter Rowell, and we divided the Bizonia work between us. He was based in the Embassy, whereas I worked for four days a week in the Pentagon, where I shared an office with American colleagues in a small unit devoted to these German affairs. We formed a close-knit Anglo-American outfit; quite small, almost as intimate, I suppose, as the four-power Secretariat I had worked at in Berlin. It was a friendly place, and we co-operated happily despite our different national interests. I am sure that my colleagues sometimes forgot that I was not one of them. We were united by our concern to meet Germany's urgent needs. I have a pleasant memory of attending the wedding of one of my colleagues in Washington Cathedral, and of the splendid reception that followed.

After a year of the fifty–fifty agreement, there were further talks between American and British representatives to review the situation. The agreement had certainly alleviated Britain's difficulties, but the burden was still excessive, and the government hoped for revised terms that would provide further relief. I attended this meeting, and was much amused to hear one Foreign Office participant ask his neighbour, 'Why is that American woman sitting on our side of the table?' All my time spent in the Pentagon and with my American friends must have affected my accent.

The end of these talks was celebrated with a splendid lunch. Forty to fifty people were there, sitting around flower-bedecked tables in the Mayflower Hotel. The Secretary of State for the United States stood up and opened his speech of welcome with 'LADY and Gentlemen...' A few years before I would have wanted to crawl under the table with embarrassment at being so singled out, but I was used to being so singular by now, and just smiled and was not even slightly put out. At the end of the lunch, a senior civil official in the Pentagon called over one of the waiters, pointed to the floral decorations, and asked,

'Have we paid for these flowers?'

'Yes, sir,' said the waiter.

'Well, I want you to put them all in the back of my car. I'm going to send them home with this lady.'

So he did. Our house was absolutely overflowing with flowers. When I left Washington in 1949, he wrote a charming letter saying what a pleasure it had been having me in the office, and how I had done more than I could have guessed for Anglo–American relations.

Around this time, serious anxieties began to arise about nuclear espionage and the suspected leakage of very secret information to the Soviet Union. It was feared that there might be an agent in Washington, and British authorities sent a spycatcher to investigate. He called in each of the Embassy staff to question them about their work and their personal contacts. I was asked about my access to secret papers in the Pentagon, and also about the Russian contacts I had made while working in Berlin. I could be of little or no help to them, but there was a man in the Embassy who certainly could, though he had not been detected at the time: Donald Maclean. He and Guy Burgess, two members of the Cambridge Spy Ring, defected to the Soviet Union in early 1951. This explained something strange I had noticed about Maclean. He had the world at his feet: he was senior, youngish, handsome, and popular, with a delightful wife. Strangely, whenever I saw him around the Embassy, I wondered why he always seemed such a bundle of nerves. Later I realized this must have been the strain of living his double life.

The Pentagon, the American equivalent of Britain's Ministry of Defence, was a few miles outside Washington. General Leslie Groves of the Engineering Corps, who was later the military Chief of the Manhattan Project, was the man responsible managing the construction of this extraordinary building, squat in form, consisting of an external pentagon with four concentric inner rings. The Pentagon had been built very quickly, completed in 1943, and was still new when I worked there.

It was the size of a small town, with a busy underground bus station where the bus lines that brought the staff to work converged. A vast network of new roads met beneath the structure, and the underground section contained a shopping mall, so you could go to a bookshop in your lunch hour, or buy the latest fashions from Lord & Taylor. There were numerous restaurants; there was even a hospital. It was said that you could be born in the Pentagon, work there all your life, and never emerge until you were carried out in your coffin.

The Pentagon was quite cut off from the outside world, and the inner offices had no windows. The ventilation and lighting were said to be so scientifically perfect that there was no need for windows, but the sickness rate was high, and I believe that it was eventually decided to mitigate staff claustrophobia by painting fake windows on the walls disclosing *trompe l'oeil* landscapes.

There were staircases, lifts and even escalators, but movement from one floor to another usually meant walking up massive ramps. The messengers cycled up and down these ramps, delivering mail all over the building. If you arrived by bus, as I did, you got out below the building and made your way up the great ramps from floor to floor. When you got to know your way around, you could take short cuts up small internal staircases. Once I fell on one of these, wrenched my ankle, and was transported down the ramps on a gurney for treatment at the hospital below.

There cannot have been anything like it anywhere else on Earth. The contrast with the British Embassy in Massachusetts Avenue was vivid. The Pentagon was so utilitarian, so lacking in aesthetic pretension, just a huge, squat concrete building, albeit of a novel design. The Embassy was like a great and gracious English country house, designed by the famous architect Lutyens, with beautiful gardens.

At that time, Washington was a charming city, rather more so than now, with no Beltway. It resembled a quiet old Southern town, elegant and gracious, except for the run-down areas where the poor black population lived, and where white citizens seldom penetrated. The apartment in which I lived when I first arrived overlooked a park in a beautiful valley, but when I proposed to walk there, my landlady forcefully advised me that no white woman was safe there, so I never did. With time, I grew more confident. Unlike most Americans, I walked a great deal around the city, as I had done at home in London. Some of my friends were scandalized by such reckless behaviour, which they thought most dangerous. On a couple of occasions I walked to a monastery on the outskirts of Washington where the grounds contained spectacular life-sized replicas of the Catacombs, with the tomb of St Cecilia, and the Grotto at Lourdes. To get there, I walked through a poor black neighbourhood. The streets were lined with decrepit houses, and populated with children at play in the gutters and groups of shabby men chatting on the sidewalks. They were surely surprised to see a white woman walking alone, but I never found them anything but polite and pleasant, as they greeted me with an 'Evening, ma'am.'

I heard later that some of the children in this poor part of the city had reason to be grateful to one British Embassy worker, an elderly black man who was employed as a cleaner. He had no family and lived unofficially in the boiler room, spending his leisure time and most of his pay on helping these deprived children.

I was shocked when travelling by bus, to find that if it was full, and white people were waiting to board it, the conductor would order black passengers off to make room for them.

In 1948 a huge national Episcopalian Conference was held in the big neo-Gothic Washington Cathedral, which was then unfinished; the west end was still scaffolded, and walled with corrugated iron. Representatives came from parishes all over the US, and I worked as a volunteer organizing accommodation for the event. On the first evening I was on duty in the office where the delegates came to register. A very courteous black priest from New York came to the desk to ask me about his hotel booking, as the hotel could find no record of it, and all the accommodation was full. I checked my records, and assured him that the booking had been made and confirmed. When I rang the hotel, the manager sharply reproached me for having booked a room for a black visitor without mentioning his colour. As a result they had allocated him a room in error. Protest was unavailing.

I was then living with the family of my Embassy colleague, Colonel Rowell. Failing to find any alternative accommodation, I rang the Rowell family and arranged to bring the priest home for the weekend. I would sleep on the living room sofa and he would have my bedroom. They were delighted to co-operate, and so he stayed with us and was a most welcome guest, especially to their small boy who called him 'my chocolate friend'. Soon after this they were strongly criticized by an American neighbour for their action, and told that were it not for their diplomatic status, their landlord would have required them to leave. I was surprised and shocked by this evidence of blatant racism.

There was so much about the United States that I enjoyed and admired, but there were also many things which I found intolerable. Although I received more than one offer of a job there, I knew I did not wish to live there permanently.

The city was most attractive, with its parks, its abundance of trees, including many flowering cherries, its handsome buildings, and no sign of industry. It was especially lovely in the spring, but in summer it was often uncomfortably hot and humid, and traditionally, everyone who could would retreat to the New England countryside. I remember seeing elegant guests at an Embassy garden party who quickly showed most inelegant stains of perspiration on their expensive suits and dresses.

Soon after the conference in the Cathedral I decided to leave my lodgings with the Embassy family in Chevy Chase and found a house at 3202 P Street NW in Georgetown, the lovely old colonial part of Washington. It was a handsome white-boarded house dating from the early nineteenth century, with four bedrooms and a small walled garden at the back. I invited some girls from the Embassy to join me. Doris and Barbara, the Ambassador's secretary, had been living in rented rooms, and welcomed the opportunity to have the run of the house and its stone-flagged back yard. Doris brought her piano out of store, and proceeded to practise Bach's *Chromatic Fantasia* relentlessly. On summer evenings we would sit out in the garden, surrounded by morning glories and flickering fireflies. I very much enjoyed the freedom to come and go that came with living in my own house, and stayed there happily until I left Washington in 1949.

LORNA RAINBOW

'A Vital Cog'

Years later, one of my sisters was amused to find a yellowed press cutting from the *Baltimore Sun*, about a young woman diplomat in the British Embassy, described as 'a Vital Cog in the Diplomatic Wheel in D.C.' It described my career in triumphant terms, adding as a homely touch that my housemates and I grew our own tomatoes and did our own laundry.

While I was in Washington, I joined the choir at St Agnes Church. The church had a fine organ, and it was good to be part of a musical group again. The director of the choir was Robert Arnold, who was a skilled organist, and enthusiastic musician. We struck up a friendship, and played records and attended concerts together. Robert had never been to England, but was fascinated by the image of England, its old churches, traditions, and musical heritage. He had served in the US Army at the end of the War, so he was eligible for a GI Grant to fund his further education. I encouraged him to apply to the Royal College of Music in London, to study as an organist and a composer, which he

did. He was accepted, and I provided him with introductions to my
friends and family in London.

Apart from occasional visits to New York, I took little opportunity
to travel around the United States. Instead, my leisure time was filled
with Washington activities. The city was then somewhat deficient in
theatres and concert halls, although it had a beautiful art gallery which I
often visited. There were also many intimate recitals and other
interesting events. I remember attending a poetry reading by T. S. Eliot
at the Library of Congress. After my high expectations, I am sorry to
say that I found his mournful appearance and sepulchral voice
thoroughly depressing.

My time in Washington coincided with a most historic occasion:
the signing of the North Atlantic Treaty in April 1949. It was not
possible for all the Embassy staff to attend the ceremony, and so we
drew lots for tickets, and I was fortunate enough to receive one. I was
aware that it was a momentous occasion, but I knew very little about it;
unlike the Marshall Plan, which provided American aid to help restore
post-war Europe, it did not affect my own work in any way. Like most
other people, I had little idea of the future importance of NATO.

To the career-driven young woman of today, it may seem hard to
understand why I resigned from my diplomatic post in Washington in
the summer of 1949 to return to England, although it seemed clear
enough to me at the time. As the successful restoration of Germany
proceeded, and the period of occupation drew to an end, my work was
winding down, but that was not the only factor.

Demobilization, and the reorganization of a country to a peacetime
basis, happens gradually. There is a huge amount of readjustment to be
made, especially so when a country has been as comprehensively
mobilized for war as Britain had been for years. By 1949, the end of the
occupation of Germany was in sight, and the world was changing from
a wartime to a post-war situation. Life was beginning to return to what
we used to regard as normal. The clever young men who had been in
the services during the War had returned to university, and had
graduated with shining first-class degrees in 'Greats'. Now they were
reclaiming their traditional places in government departments and in
the diplomatic service. Women who had filled the gaps during the War
were generally being displaced. They were expected to return to their

former roles, and many were glad to do so. My diplomatic appointment was a temporary one. It never occurred to me to think that I had established any right to a special position in this man's world. The diplomatic service was so exclusively masculine that I doubt if it occurred to anyone else either.

Though I was reasonably confident in doing my work, I lacked confidence outside it: society at large did not encourage girls to be confident. If I wanted to continue in the diplomatic corps on a permanent basis, I would eventually need to pass the same rigorous examinations as all the bright new male graduates. I felt that I would not be able to compete with them, and did not think to discuss my situation with others at the Embassy. Nor did I know of any other women diplomats to talk to.

I had also been through many cultural shocks in the preceding ten years, and they had taken their toll. I had gone from wartime London, with its bomb damage and shortages, to the ruined city that was Berlin and the industrial desolation of the British Zone, to prosperous Washington, where the people were sleek, well fed and well dressed and where it was hard to imagine the suffering and deprivation of Europe. I found it difficult to reconcile these three contrasting worlds. Britain beckoned to me, and I wanted to go home.

With hindsight, I can see there might have been alternatives which would have let me continue my diplomatic career. At the time, I simply handed in my letter of resignation with the feeling that I had done my bit, and that it was time to go. My colleagues in the Pentagon office gave me a very warm farewell, presenting me with a handsome blue leather suitcase, which I still have, and I left for England. I had no clear plan for the future, only a sense of a job well done.

I sailed home on the *Mauritania* and was delighted to find my cabin full of flowers as a farewell gift from my friends in the Cunard office. I had a five-day voyage ahead of me, and then the home country I had left so long ago.

Back to England

Chapter 9

Family Values

In the spring of 1949, I was home again in London with my family. After my four years abroad in Berlin and Washington, post-war London seemed a world away. It was as unlike the London that I had first known as a child and then student as the London of the War had been. I did not intend to return to teaching, and I soon found what I hoped would be an interesting post with an organisation new to me: the Family Planning Association (FPA). The FPA was then only some nineteen years old. It was a voluntary organisation, run by public-spirited people, mostly women, and including a number of well-known physicians, whose object was to provide contraceptive advice and services to women who needed them. The association ran some clinics itself, but it was largely occupied with campaigning for such services to be provided throughout the country by local authorities, hospitals, and family doctors.

The world in which the FPA operated would be hard to imagine for anyone below the age of, say, fifty. There was dire poverty on a large scale. Much of the nation lived in dreadful slums, the conditions of which the more affluent members of society were only dimly aware. The NHS was in its infancy, and there were only the rudiments of a welfare state: the dole for the unemployed, and a small Old Age Pension of a few shillings. Living in overcrowded and unsanitary conditions, with children they could not afford to clothe or feed properly, many mothers dreaded the birth of another baby, and regarded a miscarriage or a stillbirth as a blessed relief rather than a misfortune. Multiple pregnancies often caused damage to a woman's health, including permanent internal injuries, and they seldom received treatment.

Though I was already aware of the widespread poverty, I was shocked by the accounts I heard in the FPA office from doctors working in the slum tenements around Euston. I heard about the especially painful effects on women and babies, the marital stress, and the damage to the mother's health caused by under-nourishment, overwork, and excessive childbirth. For many women, an illegal back-street abortion, with all its medical and legal hazards, seemed the only remedy. At the time, many doctors would not assist with women's health and family planning; they saw it as either a 'social problem' or 'not proper medicine,' or they objected to it on moral grounds as being 'wicked', and 'against the laws of God and man.' So the FPA provided one of the few sources of information and assistance for women.

Awareness of this hardship and suffering did not make the FPA office a gloomy place, quite the contrary. There was a great sense of purpose, and an atmosphere of optimism and enthusiasm. I was the General Secretary, one of the few members of the tiny office staff. There was a constant coming and going of doctors, committee members, volunteers, and visitors. Lady Gertrude Denman, the President, though seldom seen in the office, was a benign presence – shabby and eccentric. Some of the medical members, mostly women, were delightful, in particular the gentle and charming Dr Joan Malleson, wife of Miles Malleson, the Shakespearean actor. The formidable Dr Helena Wright and her equally formidable son, Dr Beric Wright were also medical members; I was quite terrified of both.

The driving force of the FPA was undoubtedly the Honorary Secretary, Margaret Pyke, after whom the present head office of the FPA in London is named. She had a striking appearance, tall and slender, glacially beautiful, with penetrating blue eyes. She was intellectually formidable, and was full of controlled energy, courteous but severe in her demeanour. I admired her intensely, but was more than a little afraid of her. She had been married to an extraordinary scientist, Dr Geoffrey Pyke, about whose wartime work much has been written. Their talented son, David, became a distinguished doctor.

The office dealt with a mass of correspondence, in particular the many letters from women of all classes asking for advice and information on a variety of family and marital difficulties. Some of the letters were very moving, filled with bewilderment or distress as the women described their circumstances. The letters were usually handled by the little group of hard-working volunteers – society women, mostly young – who came in regularly to assist with the correspondence. In the basement was the busy, brightly lit Despatch Office, where two or three cheerful middle-aged women (no girls) sat at a big table, packing condoms that had been ordered by mail. Each was carefully inspected before packing and despatch. Contraception for women could not, of course, be supplied in this way.

It was no longer the case that anyone sending family planning advice and information by post was liable to criminal prosecution (for transmitting indecent material through the Royal Mail), but those days were not long past. The FPA's activities were still decidedly controversial, and were strongly opposed by large sections of the public. The Association was careful, therefore, to disarm criticism and not arouse disapproval unnecessarily. Its clinics were open to married women only; anyone unmarried, or conspicuously young, who sought advice would be unlikely to be admitted. If one was unmarried but engaged, one might be asked to produce evidence of a wedding date in the near future.

The case for family planning was argued by the FPA spokespeople in many meetings with local authorities and other official bodies, and sometimes in public debate. The grand objective of the FPA was to end the sorry social conditions of the overburdened mothers, and to bring about a world in which every child would be a wanted child. There was a great deal of persuading to be done, and the persuaders had to break through a huge barrier of resistance, made up of principled opposition as well as prejudice, Puritanism, and misogyny. They also had to promote reasonable and well-informed dialogue in an area in which there was little or no basis for such dialogue, in a world in which ignorance of sex was universal, and practically no one ever discussed it even when they needed to. The subject was taboo, and most people did not even have the language to talk about it. All of this took place nearly twenty years before David Steel's 1967 Act of Parliament which legalised abortion, and before the invention of the contraceptive pill and its widespread availability.

On one occasion I was the speaker at the opening of a new FPA clinic, which was to be run by volunteers. I gave a brief speech. At the end of my speech, a man shouted at me, yelling that the activity there was 'against the will of God'. Unfortunately, this was a common attitude.

Occasionally, if I had a spare half hour during the working day, I would go down to the basement laboratory for a change of scene. There in his small room, the FPA fertility specialist sat quietly at his microscope, patiently doing sperm-counts. These fertility investigations were a small and seldom noticed offshoot of the FPA's work. It was a great pleasure to talk to this gentle Austrian physician. Occasionally I would be permitted to spend several minutes at the microscope, watching the intense activity of the countless minute creatures – some so strong and quick-moving, some pathetically slow and feeble. They brought to mind some lines by Aldous Huxley:

> *A million million spermatozoa,*
> *All of them alive:*
> *Out of their cataclysm but one poor Noah*
> *Dare hope to survive.*

The work of this laboratory, purely diagnostic and advisory, was ahead of its time in investigating the possible causes of infertility. It considerably predated later developments in reproductive technology studies such as artificial insemination, in vitro fertilization (IVF), and surrogate motherhood. The lab was a wonderfully peaceful place: small, dark, and filled with quiet concentration.

I wonder how the FPA pioneers would view the changes that have occurred in the past fifty or sixty years. Undoubtedly, they would all have rejoiced at the increased national prosperity, the work of the NHS, improved care for the health and welfare of women and children, the great advances made in both the availability and the medical and technical family planning methods. All would, I am sure, have been glad to see the departure of the back-street abortionists and the clarification of the law on abortion.

I believe they would have been saddened and surprised by the extraordinary number of legal abortions today. Most of them had believed that when contraception was quite easily available, the number of abortions would be quite small, and only on clearly understood medical grounds. Many of them might have considered that the contraceptive pill, so simple and convenient compared with the old-fashioned methods, was something of a mixed blessing if it was too widely available to the very young. There would have certainly been doubts about the possible side effects. The FPA's dream of 'every child, a wanted child and every pregnancy a wanted pregnancy' has not been fulfilled. Still, I doubt that any would want to turn the clock back fifty years. Every reform brings new problems as well as solutions.

My time with the FPA was briefer than I had expected. Robert Arnold, known as Bob, the American choirmaster that I had met

Lorna and Bob on their wedding day, 1949

during my time in Washington, was now living in London. We married in 1949, and the following year we started a family of our own.

I worked at the FPA office until three weeks before my first son's birth. One fine October morning in 1950, I went out for a walk in Kensington Gardens with our dog, an affectionate young Alsatian that Bob had rescued from the Battersea Dogs' Home. We enjoyed the sunshine and freedom and he raced around chasing the flying autumn leaves. In the afternoon I was taken to St. George's hospital at Hyde Park Corner, and looked forward happily to the arrival of our baby.

The event was very different from my expectations, or indeed those of the medical staff at St George's. One nervous but prescient medical student had foreseen difficulties, but his mentor, an older doctor, pooh-poohed his concerns. After two – or was it three? – horrible days, and two trips to the operating theatre, I was finally shown a small baby, tightly wrapped in a white towel, still and pale; not at all like newborn babies I had seen. He was taken away to Intensive Care, and I was put in a small private room to recover. There I stayed for a few days, weak and wretched, convinced that my baby was dead and that I was not being told. Then one night, a brave young nurse came in quietly with a small bundle. She said 'I've brought your baby, but don't tell anyone or I'll be in terrible trouble. I must take him back in a minute or two, but you needed to see him.'

We went home a fortnight later. We were both rather feeble, and poor little Geoffrey had his tiny left arm in an aeroplane splint and required daily hospital care. But, as one nurse told me, we were quite fortunate to both be alive. I later realised Geoffrey was especially fortunate to have escaped brain or nerve damage. Very soon he was a strong, healthy little boy, growing rapidly, and full of vitality.

What the future held for me as a new wife and mother I could not foresee, but clearly my life's work was not to be social betterment through family planning.

Chapter 10

House of Harpsichords

Early music for nineteenth century audiences meant Bach and Handel. The great wealth of music before their birth in 1685 was little known and less appreciated. It was unsuitable in form, content, and style to big concert halls, large symphony orchestras, modern instruments, and most virtuoso performers.

This situation began to change in the early 1890s. Small craft workshops appeared, in which copies of old instruments – harpsichords, clavichords, lutes, and others – were made. The most famous in England was the Haslemere workshop of Arnold Dolmetsch and his family. They were excellent musicians and performers, as well as expert craftsmen. The most celebrated harpsichordist of her day, the charismatic and somewhat eccentric Madame Wanda Landowska, became a star international recitalist. Connoisseurs sought out old instruments to buy and restore. By the 1950s, the movement was gaining in strength.

Among the heroes of the earlier post-war years was a dedicated instrument builder, Tom Goff, who lived in an old house in Pont Street, Chelsea with his mother. He was a tall, patrician figure, a gentle and courteous man, modest in manner to the point of diffidence. His mother, Lady Goff, devoted herself to embroidery of courtly magnificence, stitching curtains and cushions fit for an Elizabethan palace. This she often did, we heard, in the company of Queen Mary, also an enthusiastic embroideress.

Tom had a workshop at the top of his house where he worked on building harpsichords and clavichords with the utmost dedication. He was assisted by a highly skilled cabinetmaker, J. C. Cobby, who produced exquisite cases for the instruments. Tom's designs were based on old models but he introduced several new features that made his keyboards much sought after. One novel feature was the use of an iron frame instead of a wooden one, which made them stronger and less liable to go out of tune. Another was his invention of a mechanism called a 'swell' which enabled the player to vary the dynamics in a way not possible before. The workshop always had a long and distinguished waiting list.

He had many eminent friends, musicians and others, but always found time for keen young music students. He was a hero to a small group of students from the Royal College of Music, including my husband Bob. Bob and a pianist friend, Peter, were admitted to Tom's workshop where they worked hard, made themselves useful, and learnt a great deal about harpsichords and other early keyboard instruments: virginals, spinets and clavichords. Another of Tom Goff's protégés was the young guitarist and lutenist, Julian Bream. Tom gave him much encouragement and practical help at the beginning of his pioneering career. I only met Tom two or three times, but in 1950 he became very important in our lives.

At the time, lovers of early music were busy seeking out and rescuing old instruments and having them restored. Old discarded spinets and harpsichords might be found in lumber-rooms, attics and out-houses, often in a pathetic condition. Others, which had been kept by their owners as elegant pieces of furniture, had been gutted and made into cocktail cabinets. So the rescue work of the collectors was invaluable, and came none too soon. By the 1950s there were only about twenty surviving virginals, the most popular Elizabethan keyboard instrument.

One of the most comprehensive collections was assembled by a British army officer, Major Henry George Benton Fletcher. When he died in 1946, he left it to the National Trust on condition that the instruments should be maintained in playing order and should be accessible to anyone interested in early music. It was a large collection, including seven harpsichords, two spinets, two virginals and a clavichord. Most dated from the eighteenth century and had been built in England by the finest builders of the day; the earliest instrument was an Italian virginal dating back to 1548. The collection included a very beautiful harpsichord on loan from the Queen, a splendid product of the Antwerp workshop of Hans Ruckers, dated 1612. This superb two-keyboard instrument in its handsome red and black case is believed to have been Handel's harpsichord, though there is no documentation to support this.

The collection was housed in No. 3 Cheyne Walk, a tall, narrow, Georgian house in Chelsea, and was supervised by a small expert committee consisting of Tom Goff, Raymond Russell, and James Lees-Milne. They had a difficult problem. To keep such instruments in perfect playing condition is an exacting task. Unlike modern pianos, they need constant attention, frequent tuning, the regular replacement of strings, and minor repairs.

There were few people with the musical and technical skills required to maintain the instruments, and they were likely to be heavily committed already. It could not be a well-paid, full-time post, yet someone was needed who would be constantly at hand, and who would be able to meet the special demands of recitals or instrument loans.

Tom's imaginative solution was that my husband Bob should be appointed to take care of the instruments, in exchange for a rent-free flat on the top floor of the house in Cheyne Walk. Bob accepted, and with our baby son we left our shabby old flat in West Kensington and moved to a new, fashionable address in Chelsea, with a view of the Thames and Battersea Park beyond it. The housekeeper and curator, a lady formerly employed by Major Benton Fletcher, had a flat in the basement. Our flat was in the attic, and consisted of a bedroom, a small sitting room, a tiny kitchen, and a tool store. There was no bathroom, but we were to have the use of one on a lower floor. Fortunately we had very little furniture. We could not bring our piano, so it was taken to the vestry of the church where Bob was organist, and used for choir practices. To the best of my knowledge it is still there.

We loved our new little flat, and especially enjoyed the splendid view from our front window of the Thames with its yachts and busy river traffic, and beyond it the green expanse of Battersea Park. I was enchanted by the elegant old house, with its high rooms, panelled walls and polished floors. There were no ornaments, and very little furniture apart from the wonderful keyboard instruments in every room.

There would often be sounds of music from below when there were visitors during the day, or when there was an evening recital. At night the house was almost palpably silent, except when Bob was playing or working on the instruments. Each evening when he was at home he would spend two or three hours working. He would go round

No. 3 Cheyne Walk, circa 1950

the house, checking the condition of each instrument, tuning them when necessary, and doing minor repairs and adjustments.

I would often accompany him for part of the time, sitting nearby to listen and watch. Sometimes I would have little Geoffrey on my lap when he was awake, and I did not want to leave him alone in his cot. I came to know all the individual instruments like friends with very different voices and personalities. Old harpsichords with wooden frames are very sensitive to changes of temperature and humidity, and go out of tune very quickly. During a harpsichord recital, it may be necessary to re-tune the instrument during the interval, since the mere physical presence of an audience can raise the temperature sufficiently to affect the strings.

Unlike those of a piano, the strings of a harpsichord do not sound by being struck with a hammer. They are plucked by small components called jacks, which are activated by its keys. Jacks are commonly made of leather, but sometimes of quills, often from ravens' feathers. All require very careful and precise cutting, and they are much less robust than piano components, so that small repairs and replacements are needed from time to time. Bob sometimes used condor feathers, as his father in New Jersey was able to obtain a supply from an American zoo.

Bob was working very hard. At this time he had a boring office job in Kensington, was organist and choirmaster in a London church, and devoted the rest of his time to his beloved instruments. We were delighted to have this little flat, and Bob was passionately keen on the work and in love with the musical instruments, but for me, life was very solitary.

We had no neighbours, except the curator in her basement flat. I very seldom saw her, and I believe she did not approve of us, and was suspicious of what this young American might do to her precious instruments. I had gone from my very engaging diplomatic work in Washington to the more modest, but still inspiring work at the Family Planning Association, to being a mother who had little regular contact with others. Occasionally one or two music students would drift up to the top floor, but frequently I saw no one but my baby son all day long. I had books, and a gramophone with a few records, but no telephone. I could not go out of the house, or even the flat, without taking my baby with me. Walks and shopping had to be carefully planned, especially as I had to try to avoid times when the house was open to the public and visitors were likely to be coming and going.

The logistics were fairly daunting. First, Geoffrey had to be made quite secure in his playpen. Then I would go downstairs - seventy-three steps to the ground floor - take the pram out of the garden shed at the back of the house, push it through the narrow hall without touching the panelled walls, and manoeuvre it out of the front door and down a short flight of stone steps, into a small paved courtyard. Then I returned upstairs (via the seventy-three steps) to collect Geoffrey from his playpen, and carried him down to be strapped in the pram. Then at last we were out in the wide, wide world! How delightful it was to walk by the river, to cross Battersea Park, to visit the Chelsea Hospital gardens, to explore the King's Road to buy groceries, and to go to the baker's shop in Flood Street where they would give Geoffrey a long thin breadstick to gnaw.

Interior of Cheyne Walk, from a Christmas card
from Tom Goff to the Arnolds
Shows a clavichord made by Goff and J.C. Cobby

Once, and only once, I tried to simplify the procedure by taking Geoffrey downstairs to the garden shed, strapping him into the pram and pushing it through the hall to the front door. How foolish! I did not, fortunately, scratch the panelled walls, but when I came to the front door and began to wheel the pram down the flight of stone steps, I could only hang on for dear life. Just as my strength gave out, the lady from the basement appeared and averted catastrophe by helping to lift the pram and baby down into the little courtyard. I was ashamed of my stupidity and, unlike my son, very frightened.

A joyous memory of 1951 was the Festival of Britain, a national exhibition that greatly lifted the spirits of the British public after the dreary post-war years. Our bedroom windows commanded an unrivalled view of the exhibition in Battersea Park. The Festival was so beautiful, decorative and celebratory, lively and full of verve, with a quite un-British wit and elegance. The firework displays every evening were entrancing. I was anxious lest the bangs and flashes might frighten

Geoffrey, then nearly a year old, whose cot was by the window. Before the display began on the first evening, I woke him up and held him in my arms, looking out at the sky. He was wild with delight when the fireworks began. Every night he wanted to stay up for the full performance, and when the displays finally came to an end he was quite forlorn.

Though we had no neighbours in No. 3, I was well aware of the family in the house next door, No. 2. When the weather was fine I used to see Vera Brittain, author of the much-admired *Testament of Youth*, sitting with her portable typewriter on an upper floor balcony. We had a pleasant encounter with one member of the family. One evening in late 1951, Bob and I had a rare opportunity to go out together. Our son was in hospital for a few days, and after visiting him we went to a concert. When we returned home, we found a charming, fair-haired girl of student age sitting on the stone steps of our place at No. 3. She told us that she had a problem: she lived next door, her parents were away and she had arrived home to find that she could not get in, because her brother seemed to be out. Could we help?

We began by taking her upstairs to our flat, where I made a pot of coffee. We talked for a while and Bob and I, who were both very attentive to speaking voices, listened to her with special pleasure. (I still enjoy her voice to this day.) Then Bob climbed up our fire escape via a ladder onto the roof. He came back to tell us that the trap door to No. 2 was not locked or bolted, so our visitor said goodbye to me and went up the ladder. Bob, with his torch, escorted her across the leads and saw her safely into the attic of No. 2. That was my first, last, and unforgettable meeting with (now Baroness) Shirley Williams, daughter of Vera Brittain.

The logistics of living at the top of No. 3 became even more complicated after our second son, Stephen, was born in June 1952. Luckily, Stephen's birth was an easy one, a relief after the birth of my first child. I could not carry both infants while going up and down the stairs, so every venture into the outside world involved three trips up and down the seventy-three steps, and ended with four trips to convey children and shopping upstairs and then downstairs again to put away the pram in the shed. It was slow work and tiring and, of course, during all these manoeuvres I had to ensure that each child was safe and secure when left alone.

Lorna and Geoffrey in the garden of No. 3 Cheyne Walk

In spite of these difficulties, life at No. 3 Cheyne Walk was very happy, and I have joyful memories of it. Then one morning I found Geoffrey's little felt slippers by his cot, clearly nibbled by mice. A night or so later, I had a vivid dream. A small mouse came out of the wainscot and addressed me boldly. I should not, he said, resent his presence; he had a right to be here, and his family had lived in the house since it was built. We were interlopers, and we would soon be gone, while he would stay.

Indeed, it could not last. Two adults and two little children could not possibly continue to live in such a small flat at the top of a tall house, where no noise could ever be tolerated except during the 'silent hours'. As the lady in the basement had clearly seen from the beginning, and the men on the National Trust Committee had not, it had been somewhat unrealistic. But I am glad to have had the chance to live in that fascinating old house for two years, surrounded by beautiful musical instruments that I loved, though I could not play them. As it happened, we did not have to make the decision to leave, nor did the National Trust have to turn us out. The Trust received a splendid bequest: Fenton House, a handsome and spacious seventeenth-century house and gardens on Hampstead Heath. Fenton

House already contained a large and valuable china collection, and could also provide excellent accommodation for the Benton Fletcher instruments. The National Trust sensibly decided to sell No. 3 Cheyne Walk and transfer the Benton Fletcher collection to Fenton House, where it still is today.

A flat for Bob and his family at Fenton House was not practical, so it was agreed that he should receive a salary as part-time curator of the instruments, instead of free accommodation. He would no longer be living with the instruments – the Broadwood, the little Tschudi, the splendid Ruckers and the others – but would still see them several times a week. So we said goodbye to life with the harpsichords, and to Chelsea and to the ever-interesting River Thames.

Chapter 11

Uncertain Times

At the end of 1952 we left the House of Harpsichords, and made our way to our new home in Brondesbury Road, about six miles to the north. I travelled in the furniture van with the babies, while Bob walked beside us with a torch, directing the driver through the acrid, choking fog of a London pea-souper. The world was silent and occluded; there was very little traffic, and what there was crawled at a walking pace. It took hours to get to our new house, and the fog persisted for days, muffling every sound, and making the world outside seem unreal.

I settled down to family life, staying at home and caring for the children. My days were spent reading, baking, cooking, and taking the boys to the park. I also sang in Bob's church choir when I could get away. We had a neighbour who loved the smell of my baking, and asked me to put an extra loaf or cake in the oven for her. She offered to pay for it, and the money would have been welcome. When I did the maths, I discovered that the ingredients cost more than the shop price, so I gave up any idea of supplementing the meagre family income by baking.

Near our home at Brondesbury Road was a fire station. One day, I managed to lock myself out of the house. I do not remember if the lock had been just changed, or whether I had forgotten to put the key in my pocket. Both of my boys were taking a nap in the nursery, and I had gone out to the garden to hang up some washing. What was I to do? I ran along to the fire station, told them my sad story, and they said, 'Well, ma'am, we'll find a way to get you in.' They called up the police and got permission, and then in full gear, including brass helmets, they drove a fire engine the short distance to our house, just as though they were going to a fire.

The nursery faced over the street and had a little stone balcony outside the window. The firemen put up their ladder and climbed in. Geoffrey woke up and was delighted to see his helmeted friends from the fire station, which we passed nearly every day. The firemen 'rescued' the children, and then we all went into the kitchen for cups of tea and mugs of milk and slices of cake all round.

In 1953, a legacy from my Uncle Aubrey enabled me to put down a deposit on a house in Oxgate Gardens, a few miles further to the north. Bob had now moved on from his boring office job, and was working in the engineering and management of radio broadcasts and studio recording. He worked for a time at the BBC, where he was a studio manager for *The Goon Show*, and for World Service programmes. Then he joined EMI as a recording engineer, where he specialized in recording classical music. He recorded some of the great musicians and singers of the time, including Sir Thomas Beecham and the great soprano Elisabeth Schwarzkopf. His work meant that he had to travel, sometimes abroad. During this time, he was also involved in the development of stereophonic sound and the new Long Playing (LP) vinyl records.

We had many musical friends, including Sybil Goldfoot, the wife of our kind family doctor. She was an accomplished pianist with a fine singing voice. Bob persuaded her to concentrate on singing; he suggested to her that the music colleges were turning out good pianists in quantity but a beautiful voice combined with excellent musicianship was a rare gift. He asked Mary Jarred, a well-known operatic contralto, to take Sybil as a pupil, although Mary did not normally teach. Sybil soon developed a successful career as a mezzo-soprano and won critical acclaim under her professional name, Sybil Michelow.

In spite of many happy times together, I realized that our marriage was precariously based. If we had both been able to have separate professional lives and share a home, it might have been a lasting partnership. Bob had longed for a home and family, but his homosexuality pulled him in a different direction. It was not, as he had hoped, a passing phase, but a part of his identity.

In 1953, I needed to have a hysterectomy. I was in my late thirties, and my health had deteriorated after the birth of my second son. Auntie Phyl came to take charge of the boys while I was away, and I had the operation in the hospital at Northwood. The hospital wards

Bob Arnold at the recording controls in EMI's Abbey Road studios
early 1950s

there resembled huge aeroplane hangars, heated by gigantic coke stoves, three down the middle of each long ward. They were kept going night and day, but the man who fed them would often go on a bender, and then the stoves all went out. No one else knew how to look after them, so the nurses in their cotton frocks would run around fetching extra blankets to go on the very high beds. It was so cold!

I was in the hospital for several weeks with a post-operative infection and haemorrhages. Eventually I went to convalesce at a home in Torquay run by nuns. It was a beautiful place, and the nuns were very kind. If I had not been so worried and longing for the children, I could have had a lovely holiday.

Eventually I was able to go home again, but I was very frail. I could not pick up the children, or even last the day, so Auntie Phyl stayed on to help. She was now in her early 60s, and had retired from her office. I was very grateful – although perhaps not grateful enough – to her for her help. Bob was home less frequently, as his work continued to include a lot of travel.

One day, when Bob was away on what I thought was a business trip, I received a letter from him, saying he was on a ship on his way back to America. It was a very sad letter, but a loving one. He told me he could not cope with life in England any more. Dearly as he cared for me and for the boys, he felt the only option for him was to go back to America and look for work.

Life was hard for him on his return, but eventually he resumed his recording career, working with great classical musicians, as well as popular jazz acts such as Count Basie and Ella Fitzgerald. He even won a Grammy for recording a live Judy Garland performance, called *Judy at Carnegie Hall*. Bob and I exchanged letters, remained friends, and even visited one another on a few occasions, but for all practical purposes, he was gone, leaving me a single parent, wholly responsible for my family, and without any income. I would have to get a job.

I walked down our street to Edgware Road, and passed the biscuit factory on the corner. There was a notice on the gate saying HANDS WANTED, so I went in. The receptionist was a pleasant woman, polite but suspicious.

'Are you a journalist?' she asked me.

'I need a job,' I replied, 'close to home. And I need it now. I may not stay very long.'

'Not many do,' she replied, and I was in.

I started the next day, working on a packing line. Standing all day was not ideal, as I was still sometimes weak, but I was earning money. I was fascinated to see how it all worked: the biscuits poured down from the baking department on to a conveyor belt; on either side of the belt was a long counter, with a row of women standing facing the belt. They would lift down a tin from overhead, snatch up handfuls of biscuits from the belt, and fill the tin in the correct pattern with nimble fingers. Those nearest the top of the line could fill the most tins, so positions were rotated to give everyone an equal chance to add to their basic rate of pay.

Sometimes the line would be stopped for reasons beyond our control. Towards the end of that hot summer, we were packing chocolate fingers into small, decorated tins for Christmas. As it got hotter the biscuits stuck together and we had to stop the line and do something else until the weather cooled.

Over the two months I was there my pay improved with my increasing dexterity, though I never approached the wonderful speed and skill of the old hands. It was not possible to talk on the job, because of the noise from the machinery, but I did learn something of their lives – the young Irish woman, for instance, who had left her children with their grandmother and come to England with her husband where they did four jobs between them, earning the money to buy a house back home. I never regretted my biscuit job, and the insights it gave me into such different lives, and when I finally found better paid clerical work, my sons very much missed the broken biscuits that I used to bring home.

The next few years sometimes felt directionless, apart from my determination to provide for the family. I had a variety of jobs, some more interesting than others. Auntie Phyl continued to care for the boys while I worked. We sometimes visited my parents, who had retired and were living in Lymington, and the boys would enjoy going out with my Father on his sailing boat, the *Samaki*. There was always a sense of uncertainty; would I be able to make enough to keep things going? Despite the loving support I got from Auntie Phyl and my family, there were times when I felt very alone.

For a while, I had a job at the British Institute of Management in Piccadilly. Management continued to interest me, after my introduction to the subject at the War Office, but I realized I would need qualifications to rise in that profession, and family responsibilities left me no time for study. Then I moved on to the Spastics Society, where I was their committee secretary. At that time, the Society was just a small family support group, but it was rapidly expanding thanks to the efforts of its brilliant chairman, Ian Dawson-Shepherd. A high-powered advertising executive, he was also the father of a child with cerebral palsy, and he put all his spare time into promoting the interests of children with cerebral palsy and their carers.

Geoffrey and Stephen at Lymington with their grandfather, Ken Rainbow

Shortly after I arrived, a new director came on the scene, Dr Stephens, who further enhanced the Society's work. The Society had several functions: increasing awareness of the needs of affected children, who had hitherto been regarded as 'subnormal' and shut away in institutions; providing a number of residential homes for the children and sheltered workshops for when they got older; operating day centres and special schools; and sponsoring and assisting social and medical research. Public prejudice against such children was great: one of the workers taking a child to a day centre told me she had actually heard a passer-by say 'What a disgrace to see children like that outside!'

The Spastics Society did much of its work with local authorities, co-operating closely with Social Services departments. It was very interesting, and I would have gladly worked there for the rest of my life. Unfortunately, the organization was too small for me to advance by promotion, and I did not have the right qualifications for any of the other openings there, so I left – regretfully – after two years.

I next went to work for the Federation of Business and Professional Women's Clubs. The job of General Secretary looked congenial and interesting – how nice to be working for bright, active women. I thought I had found my niche, but sadly I had not.

The Federation was run largely by the 'Honorary Members' in their spare time, and they did it as a hobby alongside their day jobs. My role was to make sure the office staff carried out the wishes of the

Honorary Members: running the business side, organizing the big annual conference as well as the regular meetings and dealing on a daily basis with a large volume of correspondence with dozens of local branches and individual members. The conferences would last two or three days, and I was responsible for every last detail: booking and allocating the accommodation, editing and circulating the papers, minuting the meetings, and doing the accounts – all under the hypercritical eyes of the Honorary Officers.

My working days were often long. At 6pm or soon after, the Honorary Secretary would be arriving from her business office, and would spend the evening planning the next conference. She would bring expensive shop-bought sandwiches; I would make more instant coffee, and prepare for two hours' hard work. She would be enthusiastically engaged in her favourite hobby, while I would be longing to go home to my two little boys, now eight and six years old.

Since my days at the War Office, I was used to hard work, but I had known what the work was for. At the Spastics Society, whatever the limitations of the organization, it was easy to see what good it did. After I left, it went on to be the big and highly successful charity now known as Scope. Now I found that the Federation of Business and Professional Women's Clubs was demanding a similar amount of effort – but what, beyond boosting the members' egos, was the purpose? There might be some point in working for the women's movement to improve the law, or to gain women access to employment, such as in the medical profession, but here I felt I was doing nothing useful.

One summer day in 1958, sitting at my desk in the dim office of the Women's Federation in Russell Square, I contemplated a pile of tedious reports and correspondence, a cheese sandwich brought from home, and a cup of instant coffee. I felt that I had to escape from the office for half an hour, so I abandoned my lunch and walked into Russell Square and sunshine. As I walked, a side turning that I had not noticed before caught my eye, and in it was a welcome sign, *Caffè* – Italian coffee bars were just beginning to appear in London. I hurried towards it, and came face to face with a familiar figure. Charles Plumb was a benign, middle-aged civil servant whom I had met in Berlin twelve years before, and had not seen since. We were greatly surprised to see each other.

Together we went into the Italian coffee bar for lunch and conversation. He asked me all about my time since the Berlin days, and about my present work; he hoped that I had found an interesting and satisfying job. I told him that I was most unhappy but it seemed I had little hope of finding more satisfactory employment, as interviewers were reluctant to select a single mother with two small children, who, as one interviewer told me, did not look strong enough to stand up to a hard day's work. I was no longer ambitious, but only anxious to find some post that would enable me to support my family.

He told me that his department, the Ministry of Health, was having staff difficulties because two women Principals had left to start families, and that it was very difficult to replace them either by promotion within the department or by trawling other departments. He thought I was just the sort of candidate required, and asked me to meet him the next day, bringing my curriculum vitæ and testimonials.

We met the next day as arranged, and very soon I was invited to the Ministry's office, in Russell Square, to see the Director of Establishments[1]. He was a charming and very clever man, who had been a star performer at Bletchley Park during the war. We got on famously and he wanted to recruit me immediately, but said he would have to seek Treasury approval, which he thought would be forthcoming in the circumstances, but it was not. He then asked me if he might send my papers to a friend and colleague who was Director of Establishments at the United Kingdom Atomic Energy Authority, which was then undergoing a massive reorganisation and expansion as a result of a serious accident in October 1957, at the Windscale nuclear plant. I gratefully accepted his help, although I was not hopeful: I could not imagine why there should be any chance of a job for me in this mysterious scientific organisation.

Much to my surprise I was called for an interview within a few days. I explained to the friendly Director that I knew nothing at all about science and could not possibly be of any use to them, but he said that my experience of committee work and writing reports and briefs was exactly what he needed. There had been three high level

---

[1] The Civil Service term for what became Personnel and later, Human Resources.

investigations of the 1957 accident by powerful government committees, and there were still important studies in hand, which required strong secretariat skills.

He warned me that before I could start work I would have to go through a rigorous security clearance process, as much of the work would be confidential or secret. The rate of new recruitment necessary to bring the organisation up to the recommended strength meant that the security staff were overloaded, and clearances were proceeding quite slowly.

It sounded interesting, and I was cautiously hopeful, but I still could not believe that I could be so lucky. My self-confidence, never strong, was at a low ebb. I was forty-two years old, late to start a new career, and with all my responsibilities I felt I could not afford to fail. Nevertheless, in December of 1958, my appointment was confirmed and I was overjoyed, if somewhat fearful.

The job itself was full of promise. I would be working in the Government Service, in a new and exciting organisation which was large enough to offer a variety of work and perhaps, even some interesting career opportunities. I could look forward to decently paid employment for years to come, and even the prospect of a retirement pension, a most surprising idea to me after a series of jobs with no such prospect. And then, even before I started work, I received another letter telling me that my starting salary would be increased, since women's pay rates in the civil service were newly being brought into line with men's – another straw in the wind of change in women's lives. I could never have foreseen how radically this new job would change my life.

It is strange that it all depended on a very small event, on my decision to go for a walk at lunchtime. If I had stayed in the office, or if I had been a few minutes earlier or later, or if I had walked in another direction, I would have not have met my old colleague, and my life would have been utterly different.

I could only exclaim, with Dante, 'Oh Fortuna!'

New World

Chapter 12

Alpha, Beta, Gamma

O n the morning of January 2, 1959 I walked down Lower Regent Street to Charles II Street. If I had turned right I should have found myself back in my familiar haunts – St. James' Square, with Norfolk House, Chatham House and the London Library. But my Norfolk House days had been fifteen years ago, in 1944. Instead I turned left from Regent Street towards Haymarket and found the London Office of the United Kingdom Atomic Energy Authority (UKAEA, but for convenience referred to from now on as AEA). It was a pleasant, modern building of modest proportions.

Inside, the atmosphere seemed friendly. In a brief interview with my new boss I was given a bewildering amount of information about the meaning of atomic energy, its immense potential for the country's future success and prosperity, and the complex, highly decentralized organization which was the AEA. Then I was introduced to a 'clever young man who has just joined us from the Treasury' with whom I was to share an office.

Ken Binning, then about thirty, was friendly and hugely enthusiastic. He had been learning fast for the previous three months, and promptly began my education. He started with a little rudimentary science, then moved on to the AEA itself: its pre-history, its creation by statute in 1954, its programme and purposes, both military and civil, and the nine nuclear sites, all new since 1946, established from the Thames Valley to the far north of Scotland.

In the late 1950s a new era in world history had been initiated by atomic science. It dominated people's minds to a degree which is impossible to recapture fifty years later. What was the potential of this incomprehensible new power, first revealed to all by the 1945 atom bombs dropped on Japan? Could it destroy human life on this planet? Could it make future wars impossible? Or could it be used for peaceful ends – to give us, in Churchill's words, 'a perennial fountain of world prosperity'? How could it be controlled, and how could it be used safely? This world-changing new science and all its implications occupied many people's minds after World War II, especially at the AEA. No wonder that nuclear power – military and civil – was so high on the government's agenda, or that the chairman of the AEA, Lord Edwin Plowden, was a constant visitor to 10 Downing Street.

Among scientists there was in general an immense enthusiasm and hope: a belief that the atom could be redeemed, and atomic power developed for purposes not destructive but beneficial. Nevertheless, as post-war governments hedged their bets, the AEA had both military and civil programmes and objectives.

It was a busy and intellectually exciting time to be in the AEA, even for a novice like me. The five years from 1955 to 1959 had been particularly eventful. Britain completed a successful series of nuclear bomb tests in Australia and Christmas Island in the Pacific, becoming the world's third nuclear power after the US and the USSR. Twelve years after the US had abrogated its wartime nuclear relationship with Britain, the British succeeded in renewing the partnership in a historic bilateral agreement which is still in force after fifty years, and has been a key element in the Anglo–American 'special relationship', which was more special to the British than to the Americans.

In 1955, following an original plan devised by the AEA, the Conservative government announced a national programme of civil nuclear power, the first in the world, consisting of twelve nuclear power stations to be built over the next decade. Then, in October 1957, the world's first big reactor accident occurred, in one of two reactors built at Windscale in Cumbria to produce bomb material.

There was indeed a great deal to learn, and it was absorbingly interesting. I was very lucky to find myself in the Authority's Health and Safety Branch (AHSB), which had been rapidly expanded following the Windscale accident only a few months before. The Health and Safety Branch was responsible both for the safety of those who worked for the AEA, and for researching and recommending standards for those working with radioactive materials. It had an Engineering

Division in the north of England, and a Radiological Protection Division at Harwell near Oxford, with a small administrative staff in London. For me, there was a great deal of unfamiliar scientific work to be studied, and very frequent contact with both the engineers and the scientists: vastly more than if I had been posted to Accounts or any other such branch.

What was so exciting about this particular period is that everything was so new. Before the war the only radioactive materials in use were tiny amounts of radium. Gram quantities of this mysterious and precious substance were shared internationally among a few scientists, and its use was almost entirely medical. In this new atomic age, novel radioactive materials were being produced in many varieties and greatly enlarged quantities, and the problems of radiological safety were immensely increased.

A great deal of research was being done on the different kinds of radiation: X-rays, so long in medical use; alpha (which could be stopped by a sheet of paper); beta (more penetrating); and gamma (which required heavy shielding). Radiological safety required much research into effective means of detection and measurement; new instruments and new units of measurement had to be developed; the *rad* and the *rem* and the *roentgen* served this purpose for some years but were later replaced by new units. I well remember the dismay and confusion the change to *sieverts* and so on caused among the older scientists!

A new post-war problem was the difficult question of internal radiation. If minute quantities of radioactive materials were inhaled or ingested, they could remain in the body, continuing to irradiate it, and in some cases causing serious long-term damage. Different radioactive materials tend to accumulate in different organs with differing effects. For example, there are bone-seeking isotopes, and others that lodge in the blood. Some isotopes decay in only hours, while others take more than a lifetime to decay. The whole subject was therefore highly complex. The work was focussed on the detection and measurement of radiation, research into biological effects (usually in the form of cancer), the establishment of safe levels of exposure, and the provision of effective methods of protection of workers and the general public.

Of course, apart from man-made sources of radiation, people are all inescapably surrounded by a sea of natural radiation from the cosmos and from the earth itself. Most of the harmful effects of low-

Lorna in the early 1960s

level radiation exposures – cancers of various kinds – are stochastic; that is, the dose received suggests the *probability* of a negative result, not the *severity*.

Once I had arrived at the AEA, I was immediately put to work with a scientist from Harwell to serve on the Veale Committee on Training in Radiological Safety, reporting to the government on the urgent need for highly qualified staff to deal with post-war nuclear health and safety problems. The Veale Committee was a memorable experience. I began work with the advantage of the techniques I had learnt in the Army Council Secretariat, and they served me admirably. The subject matter was extremely new and very challenging, especially for a scientific newcomer like me.

The committee included distinguished scientific members, whom I quickly got to know and admire, and our work entailed visits to laboratories, hospitals, and nuclear sites around the country to see the work in progress and to discuss the health and safety aspects with the scientific and engineering staff.

One scientist whom I met was Sir Ernest Rock Carling, an eminent surgeon and radiation expert, then in his eighties. As we both lived in London, he would give me a lift to the sites we visited, and it was a privilege to listen to his discourse as we travelled wrapped in rugs in the back seat of his big car. He talked about his long career from the early days of radiology. As a surgeon he had pioneered the medical uses of radiation. From him I gained a feeling for what the whole exciting and fascinating project was about, and how it had developed. At first I was intimidated by his age and eminence, but he was so interesting and kind that we became good friends. After his work on the Veale Committee came to an end, I would sometimes visit him at the Ministry of Health, where he was a part-time consultant.

Another notable scientist who became a greatly valued friend was Professor Val Mayneord, a radiation specialist and close associate of Sir Ernest. At that time a slight, auburn-haired man in early middle age, Val was not only a brilliant scientist; he was a man of varied gifts – witty, widely read, a good amateur musician, an expert on Italian Renaissance art and a devoted student of Dante.

Though exchange of nuclear information between the United States and Britain had abruptly ended in 1946, the field of health and safety was an exception. An international body, the International X-ray and Radium Protection Committee, had been set up in 1928 to study radiation hazards, which then occurred almost exclusively in hospitals. This committee had been in abeyance during World War II, but had been revived in 1950 as the International Commission on Radiological Protection (ICRP) by a few scientists and doctors, with Rock Carling and Mayneord taking the lead, with an American scientist, Dr. Karl Morgan. These concerned scientists and doctors were acutely aware of the immensely increased range and scale of nuclear hazards in the post-war world. The ICRP was the creation not of governments but of a few international scientists and medical men from the United States, Britain, France and Scandinavia. It acquired an authoritative voice and was successful in developing radiation safety standards which were accepted worldwide. Its sister organization, the International Commission on Radiation Units (ICRU) was also developing improved ways of measuring radiation – an indispensable factor in its control and safe use.

In the early days of X-rays, the only measure of patient exposure to radiation was the 'erythema dose' – the amount of exposure that caused a reddening of the patient's skin. Val Mayneord told me about his experience as a young hospital physicist (a new calling at the time) when he saw the radiation burns on breast cancer patients, and of his consequent determination to devote himself to improving the measurement and control of radiation.

The more I learnt about this absorbing and very important subject, the more I felt that I was hugely fortunate to be engaged in it and to be working in this extraordinary new world. It was such a satisfaction to me later in life to see how successful the work of developing safety standards had been, in spite of the unavoidable scarcity of information. If the scientists had got the standards wrong because of incomplete data there could have been serious consequences.

Spirits were high in the Health and Safety Branch. There was so much new and important work being done, so much collaboration with other scientists and doctors at home and abroad, such satisfaction in an activity that was unequivocally directed to human well-being, and with so many good people doing it. Our work was intellectually exciting and full of hope.

The Scientific Secretary of the Veale Committee, Ted Johnstone, was an excellent colleague, kind and funny and very helpful in my scientific education. I particularly remember an enjoyable working trip to Belfast, when we visited Stormont and Queen's University. We worked well together, the Committee gathered momentum, and it made its report early in 1960. Since the others soon realized I could draft pretty well, I took a full part in writing the report. It was published as a substantial Command Paper[1], and made many detailed recommendations, most of which were accepted in full. One recommendation – the setting up of the National Radiological Protection Board (NRPB) – was delayed by some ten years, apparently on grounds of cost.

Soon after the report was published, a seminar on radiation safety was held in Oxford, and the proceedings were recorded. I had been

[1] *Report of the Committee on Training and Radiological Health and Safety* (HMSO, 1960)

unable to attend, so Ted found a quiet corner in a small Oxford laboratory, little more than a cupboard, to play back the tape he had made of the proceedings. One very witty speaker had drawn much laughter and applause from a delighted audience, and we joined in the merriment. Presently there came a knock on the door of our hideaway. We opened up to find a famous Oxford scientist standing outside with a puzzled look on his face. 'Vot is happenink here?' he asked. 'I pass by a broom cupboard and I hear a crowd clappink and laughink – where are all the people?'

The Windscale accident continued to be a source of concern, and particularly the health of the many workers who had been involved in the cleanup. In the early 1960s, I suggested that it would be interesting to follow up the health records of these workers compared to a control group, but the Director thought it would be infringing their privacy to do so. Many years later, in the 1980s and 1990s, the Society of Radiological Protection did exactly that. They matched the Windscale workers with a control group and found the incidence of cancer almost exactly the same in both groups: they had suffered no harm from being involved in the cleanup. The editor of the *Journal of Radiological Protection*, published by the Society of Radiological Protection, invited me to contribute an article on the topic. This was only one example of the good judgment which the scientists of the 1950s and later had shown in setting standards and procedures for the safety of radiation workers.

Henry Arnold was another friend whom I first met due to an odd chance: our shared last name. I would occasionally receive mail that was addressed to him, and bring it to his office. As we got to know one another, we discovered that we shared an interest in art, and we would visit exhibitions together. Arnold had been the Director of Security at Harwell in 1949, when Klaus Fuchs was under suspicion as a spy for the Soviets. Arnold persuaded him to speak with a member of MI5, and this eventually led to Fuchs's confession and conviction for espionage.

Klaus Fuchs had a fascinating story. He was a German émigré to Britain, had Communist affiliations in the 1930s, and was an exceptional scientist who worked with the noted physicist Professor

Rudolf (Rudi) Peierls. After being interned at the start of World War II, Fuchs was invited to join Peierls and other British scientists in the US, where they worked in the Manhattan Project, which culminated in the atomic bomb. During the War, Fuchs passed nuclear secrets to the Soviets, feeling that as our allies, they had a right to the knowledge.

After the war, he returned to Britain, and became Head of the Theoretical Physics Division at the Atomic Energy Establishment at Harwell. He continued to pass information to the Soviets about the hydrogen bomb, though it has been contested whether that information was actually of use to them. Some of the evidence that proved Fuchs's spying was contained in the decrypted Venona telegrams[2], which were highly classified, so the government could not use them as evidence. This same group of documents contained the information that had pointed suspicion at Donald Maclean, whom I had known in Washington. Fuchs had confessed and been convicted back in 1950, long before I had joined the AEA, but I found this link from my friend Henry Arnold to Fuchs and Maclean interesting.

There were social aspects to the job as well. Soon after I joined the small London office of the AEA, a music society was started which I was quick to join. We were few in numbers, but had very enjoyable and interesting meetings. Sometimes we sang part songs written for us by Eric Sans, a composer who worked at the Treasury, and sometimes we had recitals, at one of which Ruth Dyson memorably performed on the harpsichord. Sometimes we listened to records – Tom Lehrer's songs were a special pleasure. How fortunate I was in my introduction to my strange new occupation!

For the first few years of my work at the AEA, I travelled to work by bus from our house in northwest London. Aunt Phyl continued to

---

[2] The Venona project decrypted certain Soviet communications in the 1940s. Both the US and the UK were involved in the decryption efforts. These communications revealed that there were Soviet spies in the Manhattan Project, and in several branches of the US and British governments, and were the basis for accusations against Fuchs, Maclean, Kim Philby, Henry Gold, and indirectly, Ethel and Julius Rosenberg. Because the US and UK wanted to conceal that the Soviet codes had been broken, it was necessary to find other evidence in order to bring successful prosecutions against suspected spies. The decrypted documents were made public in 1995.

live with us. Her help in caring for my two boys made it possible for me to work the long hours and undertake the travel which my job required. The house was cramped for the four of us, and in 1961 I was fortunate to inherit a house in Beaconsfield. Geoffrey and Stephen went to school in High Wycombe, while I continued to commute in to London. I also bought my first car, which made my increasingly frequent visits to Harwell much more convenient.

Once the Veale Committee had produced its report, I continued to work in the AEA Health and Safety Branch, as the Director's personal assistant. It was an ideal vantage point for observing an exciting and creative period of development in this new and important field. Andrew MacLean, the Director, was a wise and witty Scotsman, who as Chief Medical Officer had been deeply involved in the Windscale accident. He was a gifted diplomat, and expert at sorting out personal differences and inter-site and professional rivalries. One of my most interesting tasks was as Secretary of the Health and Safety Branch Management Committee, where medical, physics and engineering staff would meet regularly to discuss problems and report on work in progress. These meetings were often enlivened by quick-fire exchanges between Andrew MacLean and the Chief Medical Officer, Ken Duncan, another witty Scotsman.

One subject of concern that I remember being discussed was the possible risks to women employed in AEA laboratories, since research by Dr Alice Stewart in Birmingham had shown abnormal levels of neonatal defects in babies born to women who had been X-rayed during early pregnancy. The AEA was anxious to safeguard the health of its women employees without denying them career opportunities. After some discussion of the appropriate wording, one venerable member, Greg Marley, innocently suggested that only 'unmarried ladies' should be employed in radiation areas. He was bewildered by the hilarity with which his idea was received. We all listened entranced as Ken Duncan explained the facts of life to Greg, and then the committee settled for excluding 'women of reproductive capacity', regardless of marital status.

The Management Committee's work ranged widely over such topics as international radiation research, epidemiological data at home and abroad, development of standards, limits and methods of regulation, radiation protection, and radiation hazards to workers and to the general population.

A great appeal of working in the Health and Safety area of atomic research was that, unlike the weapons programme, it was directed entirely towards the well being of humanity. We were putting immensely important safeguards into place at the beginning of the nuclear age. The science was growing fast. Very little about the effects of radiation had been known before the War, so there was a huge body of knowledge to build up, involving wide co-operation between scientists at home and abroad.

The need was urgent but the pace of acquiring knowledge was restricted by the time it took for many radiation effects to appear. Leukaemia, for example, might develop as a result of radiation exposure within the past four or five years, but some cancers might not manifest themselves for forty or even fifty years. Research could be done to hasten the process of understanding by animal experiments, such as the 'mega-mouse' experiments undertaken in the US. The most important investigation of all was of the detailed case studies of the Japanese victims of the two atomic bombs. This work sounds cold-blooded, and I was shocked at first, but I realized that since this tragedy had taken place it would be criminally irresponsible not to learn everything possible from it. The research was a huge international study carried out by the Radiation Effects Research Foundation (RERF) – literally a life-time study.

There were hardly any known ways of controlling radiation exposure at the time, even in hospitals. More and more epidemiological studies were being undertaken which added to our knowledge.

The 1950s and 1960s were periods of great progress in radiological protection which I observed with enthusiasm. As Secretary of the Atomic Health and Safety Branch, I was very much aware of the quite varied research going on in the US, in Britain, and elsewhere. The most important was the work being done in Japan by RERF, but there were also numerous studies in other countries of groups of people who had been subject to abnormally high levels of radiation, either natural or

Andrew MacLean,
Director of the AEA Health and Safety Branch

man-made. These included patients who had received radiotherapy for ankylosing spondylitis (a disabling disease characterized by fusing of spinal joints), inhabitants of certain areas with relatively high natural radiation, such as Kerala in India, and workers in uranium mines. Because many of the effects of radiation are long term, the accumulation of statistical evidence takes a long time – perhaps as long as forty or fifty years. The amassing of epidemiological data from many studies is therefore cumulative in value.

The AHSB was concerned not only with medical and biological aspects of radiation safety; it was also greatly occupied with engineering questions, and in particular with safe design and risk assessment. At this time the methodology for risk assessment was still being developed. The lead was taken by the US, but the AEA did much independent work in this area and it was fascinating to hear the reports of the senior engineer on the Committee, Reg Farmer, on the evolution of these ideas. One important concept in engineering design and operation was 'fault tree analysis': the study of inconspicuous faults to ensure that they

did not form part of a sequence with potentially serious consequences.
This sort of analysis was neatly summed up in the old rhyme:

> *For want of a nail the shoe was lost*
> *For want of a shoe the horse was lost*
> *For want of a horse the rider was lost*
> *For want of a rider the battle was lost*
> *For want of a battle the kingdom was lost –*
> *And all for the want of a horseshoe nail!*

In addition to these wide concerns, the Committee was occupied
week by week with the regular work of the AEA sites, and the health
and safety problems that arose. We followed individual cases of special
interest, such as that of one laboratory worker whose routine urine
samples indicated that he had ingested a dose of radioactive material
that was as inexplicable as it appeared dangerous. He was kept under
close medical supervision for a long time, but never apparently suffered
any ill effects. As I remember, he was identified by the popular press as
a man 'too radioactive to be allowed to sleep with his wife'.

The work of AHSB was absorbing: there was always so much new
to learn, and we had so many interesting interactions with scientists and
engineers world-wide as well as within the AEA. I enjoyed it greatly,
and hoped and expected that it would occupy the rest of my working
life. Surprisingly, it came to an end in 1967: though I did not leave the
AEA, I had to leave AHSB and pursue a new trade.

Chapter 13

Learning a New Trade

The Windscale accident in 1957, which I confess had not greatly interested me at the time, had brought me into the AEA. This accident was to be a recurrent theme in my working life for the next fifty years. In 1958, another event occurred that was to have unexpected results for me: the Public Records Act was passed.

An influential committee chaired by Sir James Grigg, formerly the wartime head of the War Office, had produced a landmark report about official records, which recommended a comprehensive system of managing the records of all government departments, and preserving those records judged to be of lasting importance in the Public Record Office in London. These recommendations were put into effect by an Act of Parliament in 1958, the Public Records Act. Those records placed in the Public Record Office (now part of the National Archives) were to be made available for public use when they were fifty years old, unless they were exempt on certain grounds such as national security.

The AEA, which had been set up in 1954, did not come within the scope of the Act, since it was not a government department, and its records and those it had inherited only went back to 1939 or 1940. Nevertheless the AEA Board wisely decided to ask that it should be included, because of the national significance and historic importance of its records. I had no idea then how this would change the course of my career, or how many years I was to spend poring over these records.

The AEA made the necessary arrangements for records management to comply with the requirements of the Act, including the establishment of the post of Departmental Records Officer. Furthermore it was decided that the successful candidate should also be asked to prepare a history of atomic energy in Britain from its beginning. This new post was then advertised, and in 1959 Margaret Gowing was appointed as AEA Departmental Records Officer.

Margaret Gowing was a young economic historian who had been working in the Cabinet Office on the official history of World War II. This project, initiated by Winston Churchill during the war, was directed by an eminent Australian historian Sir Keith Hancock, whose first reaction was to ask Churchill whether there was 'any use or point... in starting to write the history of the war before we had won it'. Churchill persuaded him to proceed, and by the end of the war, Hancock had nearly forty historians working in government departments.

In addition to her work as an official historian, Margaret Gowing had been a member of the Grigg Committee on Public Records which had led to the 1958 Act, so she was well qualified for both of the roles in her new position. Her first task was to set up a records system which would be suitable for such a decentralized organization. The AEA held a great diversity of records, many of them highly technical, and generally very unlike the official Whitehall files with which Sir Keith Hancock's historians were familiar.

The Hancock tradition was to be invaluable in approaching this new task. His historians had all been embedded in their host departments, but had been answerable only to the Cabinet Office. This meant that departments were unable to influence what the historians wrote, except where questions of fact were involved. I subsequently realized how important this guarantee of independence was, when I observed the problems that faced an American historian whose academic independence was not secured.

Margaret's first task was to organize the AEA records, and her second was to write a history of the British experience of atomic energy. When she began work in the autumn of 1959, the events she was to study were still in the fairly recent past, and many of the key participants were still alive and ready to help. So Margaret met such legendary figures as Niels Bohr, Robert Oppenheimer, James Chadwick, and Rudolf Peierls, and formed close friendships with some of them, and with others less famous. There were still no nuclear papers in the public domain, and indeed most were still classified as Secret or Top Secret. She was entering virgin territory, and had sole rights of entry.

Her first atomic book, *Britain and Atomic Energy 1939–1945*, was published in 1964. It was a sensation, since it revealed a story which was immensely important but had hitherto been kept secret. She had unique access to highly classified papers held by the AEA, which would not become publicly available for fifty years. This was indeed a new kind of history: scientific, based on classified material, and providing a tremendous insight into this new world being created by the practical applications of nuclear knowledge.

She set to work at once on the second instalment of the series, which would cover the topic of Britain and atomic energy from 1945 to 1952. By 1967 she had also obtained an academic post as Reader in Contemporary History at the new University of Kent, in Canterbury. As she was only working part-time for the AEA, it was decided to give her an assistant, and although I had no academic qualifications as a historian, the AEA chose me for the job.

It was not a role that I sought out. I had been very happy working in the AEA Health and Safety Branch with excellent colleagues, doing what I saw to be important work. I was in my early fifties, and did not feel the need for a change of career. But management felt it was important to continue both the historical work and the job of AEA Records Officer.

For the first year of my new job, I felt at a loss, and bitterly regretted my transfer. Margaret gave me one or two subjects to work on for the book and then left me to my own devices. Working very hard herself, doing two jobs and travelling between Canterbury and London, she had little time to spare for discussion. She certainly did not admire my first efforts. So while I was expected to contribute to this new kind of history, I had very little guidance.

Nevertheless, I came to enjoy the work and to develop useful techniques of my own. One of the most delightful aspects of my years at the AEA was the opportunity that I had to meet with very bright, interesting and capable people, and to have working relationships that turned into friendships. I have been very lucky indeed with the friends I made through my work.

I had also taken over Margaret's duties as AEA Records Officer. The special problems of reviewing records and physically transferring them to the Public Record Office had become more pressing after the statutory 'closed period' was reduced from 50 years to 30 years in 1967.

Margaret Gowing

The earliest records held by the AEA dated from the early 1940s, and so they would have to be transferred to the Public Record Office in just a few years, in the early 1970s, rather than in the 1990s, as originally foreseen.

This meant a great deal of work for me. The material that the AEA had was quite different from the typical Whitehall archives, the orderly 'split files' with the correspondence on the left and the documentation on the right. Of course the AEA dealt with the usual committee minutes and documents that might be found in the Ministry of Defence or in the Foreign Office, but it also had scientific records, nuclear reactor logbooks, architectural diagrams, maps, operational instructions, and many other practical materials which were associated with scientific work and the construction and administration of nuclear facilities and nuclear weapons.

The complexity of the records problem was compounded by the existence of nine different and diverse facilities, each of which managed its own records. One of the first things that I negotiated with the Public

Record Office was whether the AEA would have to submit all of its records together; fortunately, it was decided that each facility could submit material separately.

The problems associated with handling decentralized and unusually formatted records and the challenge of ensuring that secret information was not released were formidable. They demanded the detailed and coordinated review of many documents, because while certain details were not secret on their own, they could be revealing when combined with other data. In 1958, Great Britain and the US had signed the US–UK Mutual Defence Agreement, in which each agreed to exchange classified information that would enhance their ability to develop nuclear weapons. The Mutual Defence Agreement hung over our heads, as we were not only guarding our own nuclear secrets but those of our US allies. A party of US archivists visited us in London to consider the security problems that might arise, and celebrated the successful conclusion of the discussions by entertaining us to lunch at the Bunny Club in Park Lane – a novel experience, for me at least!

Many of the initial reviews of materials were performed by scientists in the various AEA facilities, who carried out this work in addition to their usual responsibilities. To help them understand the process of review, and educate the staff in our responsibilities to the PRO, I put together training materials, manuals and brochures.

Over time, we also arranged for retired senior scientists who had a broad understanding of a programme of work to review the records due for transfer. Because of the very specialised nature of the work, someone who worked solely as a chemist might not understand the implications of an engineering diagram, and so a broad understanding was required. We also had to be very proactive in advising government departments that held documents related to nuclear topics, such as the Ministry of Defence, Foreign Office and Treasury. When documents in those departments came up for review for release to the PRO, we encouraged them to engage us in the review process.

My work as the AEA Records Officer started with this urgent and pressing problem: organising the review of records which were to be transferred to the PRO to meet the mandated thirty-year review period. It continued in parallel to my work as a historian for many years. One of the advantages of this arrangement was that I became familiar with much of the material within the AEA, and had the opportunity to meet

people across the organisation as records were assessed. I also got to
know many of the senior scientific staff who served as reviewers, and
who were valuable resources to me in my work as a historian.

One side-effect of my work on AEA records was that I found
myself spending more of my time at Harwell and the Atomic Weapons
Establishment at Aldermaston and much less at the London office. The
motorway from London to Oxford had not yet been constructed, and
the daily travel became quite a burden. The house in Beaconsfield,
which had provided such welcome space as the boys were growing up,
was becoming expensive to keep up. In the mid 1970s I therefore
moved to a small house on the outskirts of Oxford, convenient for the
A34 to take me to Harwell and Aldermaston, where I've lived ever
since.

While all this was going on, Margaret and I had created a massive
second draft of the second instalment of the nuclear history, but it had
little structure to it. I proposed that we create two volumes: the first
would be on the formation of nuclear policy, and the second on its
execution. We adopted this format, created copies of the draft chapters
and sent them for review to over twenty scientists and engineers.

One of the reviewers was Christopher Hinton, the AEA Board
Member for Production and Engineering, who had been responsible
for building all the nuclear factories. He was an outstanding engineer,
and impressive personality, well over six feet tall, with aquiline features
and a commanding presence. He had had a brilliant career with ICI
before the War, and then in running the wartime ordnance factories,
ensuring that there was no breakdown in supplies such as had been a
feature of World War I.

Margaret asked me to work with Hinton on the revisions, and in
time he and I became firm friends. We enjoyed visiting village churches
together. From boyhood he had been deeply interested in mediaeval
architecture and looked at the features of old churches with an expert
eye. He would walk round the exterior first, appraising the structural
details and noting signs of damage and renovation, and would refuse to
consult the guide book until he had formed his own opinion. He would
estimate the date of the building and its subsequent history before we

Christopher Hinton

went inside. Once inside he had a keen eye for everything. One of our outings took us to Laycock, in Wiltshire, with its beautiful village and Abbey, of which he had happy childhood memories and where he was still welcomed with affection.

I was sometimes invited to stay at his Dulwich flat. When he was in his eighties, Lord Hinton spent a week at my little house in Oxford. He had just had back surgery, and was going to need help when he got out of hospital. Unexpectedly, his housekeeper was not available. When his devoted secretary asked me for advice, I offered to stay at his flat in Dulwich to help. He rang to say that he would prefer to stay with me in Oxford, and a few days later he was driven by his chauffeur to my house.

I was rather nervous but he fitted in beautifully, and we had a most enjoyable week. Despite his back he succeeded in folding himself into my small car and we set off every day on visits to local churches. In some ways, he was not an easy friend; he had a notoriously short fuse, but he was terribly kind, and we had a great relationship.

I first met Professor Rudi Peierls, the world-famous nuclear physicist, when Margaret Gowing asked me to take some papers to him at his home on Boars Hill, Oxford, not far from where I lived. I was overawed by this great man (and even more by his formidable Russian wife) but in time he was to become a close and valued friend. Rudi was born in Germany, of a Jewish family, and was studying physics at Cambridge when the Nazis came to power. In collaboration with his Austrian friend Otto Frisch, he was the first to establish scientifically that a uranium fission bomb was feasible. Early in 1940 they wrote a historic memorandum which found its way to the Government Chief Scientific Advisor, Sir Henry Tizard.

A high-powered committee was formed to consider more fully the possibilities of the Frisch-Peierls ideas. Two momentous reports, the so-called Maud Reports, resulted. In the summer of 1941 Britain passed the minutes and reports to the US, which was not yet at war. They were ignored for several months until an Australian scientist, Mark Oliphant, visited Washington and drew the attention of the physicist Enrico Fermi and others to the work. Soon afterwards the Japanese attack on Pearl Harbour brought the Americans into World War II, and they immediately set up the Manhattan Project to develop an atomic bomb, based on the Maud Report. Two years after it began, an agreement at the highest level was reached at the Quebec conference of 1943 on British participation in the project. The sixty British who eventually took part made a contribution out of all proportion to their number. Rudi Peierls himself played a vital part as head of the Theoretical Physics Division

After the War he returned to teaching and research at the University of Birmingham and later at Oxford. He was also a consultant to the AEA. Despite his eminence, he was a modest man, courageous and kind. We worked together for many years, both on books and on reducing nuclear proliferation.

In 1974, Margaret and I completed the second instalment of the atomic history. The book, entitled *Independence and Deterrence: Britain and Atomic Energy 1945–1952*, was in two substantial volumes, one dealing mainly with policy and the other with supporting material and analysis. I contributed six chapters to the book. It was very successful; even

Lorna in the 1970s

before publication, it played a part in Margaret's appointment as the first Professor of the History of Science at Oxford University.

In 1976, I received a surprising honour, an OBE[1]. When I first received a letter from St James's Palace inquiring whether I would be accepting the honour and attending the investiture, I wrote back to explain that some sort of error must have been made. I received a gracious reply, assuring me that I was indeed the intended recipient. The investiture was at Buckingham Palace, where I waited with many others in a grand ballroom, where we were coached on protocol: how to meet the Queen Mother, who was presiding at the investiture, and then how to back away respectfully after our award.

The Queen Mother was remarkable in her execution of the task; she greeted each recipient with warmth and graciousness, spoke a few personal words, assisted by an aide whispering details to her, and then

---

[1] Officer of the Order of the British Empire

turned to the next recipient with the same warmth. When informed by her aide that I was a nuclear historian, she offered, 'It must be a very short history.' While the period of time since the start of the atomic age has been short, the complexity of nuclear history has ensured that it is not brief.

Should we undertake a third instalment of the official nuclear history? The AEA Board and Margaret decided that we should, and we made our plans accordingly. The next book was to cover the years 1952 to 1959, or perhaps to 1963. I strongly favoured the shorter period, because 1959 was a more natural break point, as it was the last atmospheric nuclear test.

The work on this book went slowly, in part because of the enormous amount of material available. The two uses of atomic energy, military and civil, were developing so quickly and diverging so widely that it would be difficult to combine their history, as there were two different readerships. We pressed on with research and writing, and decided to leave the final organization until later.

As will appear, this work was destined never to be completed.

Chapter 14

Flying Solo

In the early 1980s much controversy arose in Australia about the British nuclear weapons tests that had been conducted there in the 1950s. The Australian government set up the McClelland Royal Commission to investigate the methods and effects of these tests. This all led to a great deal of discussion in the British press. Rumours and wild speculations were rife. It seemed that there was an immediate job for the AEA Historian's Office to do.

I had recently been working at the Atomic Weapons Research Establishment at Aldermaston, doing research into British weapons tests for the next instalment of the official history. I was working on a single chapter on the Australian tests: it was not enough to answer the many questions that were being asked, and it was not going to be published for several years. A separate book on the tests was needed, I thought, and as soon as possible.

The Ministry of Defence warmly welcomed the idea. I learned later that there had been great concern among ministers that nothing had been published on this subject. Somewhat apprehensively, as this was my first solo flight, I returned to work in the Aldermaston archives to create a full book on the topic. There were strict security limits, not on my research, but on what I could eventually publish.

I had three unique advantages in this task. Firstly, I had access to this vast mass of still secret material. Secondly, I was able to talk, in some cases frequently, to the scientists and others who had been involved in the tests. Thirdly, my earlier experience in the AEA gave me an invaluable background to the health and safety aspects of the tests, which was an important and controversial subject little understood by the media or the public.

I felt it my duty to do my best to produce an accurate and truthful account for the general reader; there was so much folklore and speculation in the media, so much exaggeration or misunderstanding, and so many unreliable anecdotes. I hoped that as an official historian I should not be distrusted as a company stooge.

At the same time, I felt that weapons testing was a ghastly topic. I could not help but think about the many implications of nuclear weapons, weighing their possible value as a deterrent against the horrendous implications of their use. I was familiar with the long-term studies of the effects of the atomic bombs in Japan; it was impossible to be naïve about the horrors that would occur if nuclear weapons were ever used again. Even though I continued to think about the implications of nuclear weapons, I was determined to maintain an objective approach as a historian.

Working on a single chapter about the Australian atomic bomb tests had shown me that there was a huge amount of research to do. There was a formidable quantity of material available, ranging from laboratory notebooks to Cabinet Office and other government records, and hardly any of it was in the public domain. I worked in the Cabinet Office, the Foreign Office, the Ministry of Defence, the Treasury, and above all at Aldermaston. There I found masses of scientific records and reports, laboratory notebooks, letters, photographs, maps, telegrams from test sites in the Australian desert and much, much more. There were endless newspaper reports to read. The possibilities of oral evidence were formidable; there were many scientists, not to mention some 22,000 test participants.

I was given every assistance and encouragement, especially by the Aldermaston scientists. Various people read my drafts to ensure accuracy and clear them for publication, and they were always helpful and forthcoming.

Lord William Penney, a brilliant scientist, veteran of the wartime Manhattan Project, had been Britain's chief atomic weaponeer since 1946. He invited me to his home near Harwell to discuss each chapter as I wrote it. Often he would produce information and insights which were quite new to me, and was very helpful although never overbearing. One day as he read, he exclaimed, 'Lorna, where did you get this garbage?'

William Penney

'From a Downing Street file,' I told him, 'in a minute from a Secretary of State to the Prime Minister.'

'Fellow didn't know what he was talking about!' he said.

It was a lesson to me not to take important documents at face value too readily, especially when Ministers are writing about scientific or technological matters.

Bill Penney continued to invite me to visit from time to time after the book was finished, and we had some interesting talks. I seldom asked him questions about his views, because I knew that was the quickest way to end any conversation, for he was very reticent. But he sometimes made telling comments. I remember his account of a conversation between Group Captain Leonard Cheshire and himself, as they waited on Tiniam Island to fly with the Nagasaki raid as observers of the second atomic bomb attack. They had both seen the death and destruction of two terrible world wars, and fervently hoped that this cataclysmic new weapon would draw a line across history.

I asked him why, if only a few nuclear warheads could rule out the possibility of future wars, the super powers had stockpiled weapons in thousands beyond all conceivable use, even able to destroy all human life. His answer was brief – 'Because they were mad, mad, MAD!'

Bill Penney was one of the most direct people I have ever known – he always talked in a straightforward open and friendly way whether to a Prime Minister, a naval rating, a tea lady, or a student at Imperial College, where he was later Rector. He was a sensitive man – not the Dr Strangelove that some saw him as.

Bill Penney remained a valued friend until his death in 1991, and my friendship with his wife Joan and son Christopher continued after his death. I wrote his obituary in the *Independent* which was subsequently published in the *Proceedings of the American Philosophical Society*. His funeral in the village church at East Hendred – not in Westminster Abbey, as he was entitled – was a heart-warming occasion. On the simple leaflet with the order of service was a quotation chosen by Bill himself from George Borrow.

> *Follow resolutely the one straight path before you, it is that of your good angel.*

Nothing could have been more appropriate for this good man.

He was very much loved, and a great variety of people attended his funeral in the small church. People from all walks of life and many stages of his career were present, from peers, politicians and eminent scientists to soldiers and sailors who had known him in time of war and during the post-war weapons tests. He was a keen sportsman from his schooldays, and it was said that if he had not been a first class scientist he might have been a professional footballer and played for England. It came as no surprise to find that the simple lunch that followed his funeral had been entirely provided, not by caterers, but by the people of East Hendred. It was a friendly and happy occasion, with people exchanging endless good stories about Bill. I wish I had realized earlier what a wealth of personal anecdotes about him were waiting to be gathered together – they would have made a splendid collection.

The book on the nuclear testing in Australia, *A Very Special Relationship: British Atomic Weapon Trials in Australia*, was published in 1987 by Her Majesty's Stationery Office. This was something of a disadvantage, as they did not market it well, and it was not even on sale in Australia. The cover was very colourful and one reviewer wrote that the cover was 'the only fun thing' about the book. To my relief, all the other reviews were favourable, and I was surprised and delighted by a long and appreciative review in *Nature*.

The book undoubtedly met a special need at the time, and it continues to be useful, because the weapons trials of the 1950s are still a live issue. Over fifteen years after its original publication, I was able to work with an excellent collaborator, Dr Mark Smith, of the University of Southampton, to update and extend it. The new edition included the H-bomb trials at Christmas Island, and was published in 2005 as *Britain, Australia and the Bomb: The Nuclear Tests and Their Aftermath*.

After the book on the Australian weapons tests was completed, I prepared to return to work on the third instalment of the official history. I felt even more anxious than before about the structural problems. It seemed to me that the whole subject was so large and complex that several separate books would be needed to give a comprehensive picture. Only this would ensure that important topics could receive adequate attention, and be made really intelligible to the readers.

Before I could return to work on the third volume of the 'blockbuster', the Windscale fire, a recurring motif in my life, reclaimed my attention. The accident had occurred in 1957, and in accordance with the 1967 Public Records Act, the relevant papers would be released to the Public Record Office, and to public scrutiny, in 1987. The voluminous records about Windscale were held by various government departments, as well as by the AEA. It seemed to me that if the papers were released piecemeal over several years, based on the year in which they were created, it would be impossible for users at the Public Record Office to make sense of the complex and changing story. So I arranged with the Public Record Office and the government departments involved, to make public all the papers relating to the accident in a single collection.

In order to survey and assess all the Windscale accident material that would become available to the public in the near future, I had to trace and review all the documentation. I had hundreds of AEA files transferred to Harwell, where they were stored in a former aircraft hangar while I worked doggedly through them. Additionally I visited various government departments – notably the Treasury, the Ministry of Agriculture, the Ministries of Housing and Health, the Cabinet Office, the Home Office, and Number 10 Downing Street – to get the total picture. During my meetings, I discussed the value of producing a book about the Windscale accident, which could help make sense of the material. All agreed that it was highly desirable.

My book about the accident, *Windscale 1957, Anatomy of a Nuclear Accident*, was published in 1992. It was hard work but a joy to write. It was a wonderful story to tell: the world's first big nuclear reactor accident, an exciting narrative, vivid personalities, great danger, and true heroism. There was the background of political crisis, and the long aftermath.

What a narrative this was, and what a challenge! How lucky I was to have all the records available to me, to know so many of the people involved, and to have the background of my work in the Health and Safety Branch, where the Windscale accident had been a prime concern for years.

One or two important people – not in the AEA – did not much like parts of the book when they saw it in draft. They included Margaret Thatcher, who apparently thought it shed a bad light on the conservative government of the time. Lord Edwin Plowden, who had been the first Chairman of the AEA but was now long retired, had received a copy of the draft from the AEA as a courtesy. He invited me to tea to discuss it, and courteously suggested that I should omit one chapter, which explained why the government white paper of the time had been misleading. He described it as 'pernickety' and 'unnecessary'. He admitted, though, that he was not aware of any actual inaccuracies. I told him that I could not alter it, unless I found that there were factual errors. I felt it must be my judgement as my name would be on the book. Publication proceeded, and it was well received. Some nuclear scientists and engineers who had been involved in the accident and its aftermath wrote to thank me for setting the record straight, and for refuting some persistent misjudgements of the part they had played.

I kept in close touch with some of the Windscale scientists for years afterwards. I had an interesting illustration of the usefulness of the book when I was invited to visit Windscale some years later for meetings to review progress in dismantling and studying the old reactor plant. It was an extraordinary experience to visit the old charge face and ascend nearly to the top of the 410 foot chimney, from which there was a magnificent view of the Lake District. Several of the younger recruits to the industry brought their own well-thumbed copies of my book to my hotel room to ask me to sign them. In 1995, I was asked to do a second edition of the book, bringing it up to date with all the latest developments.

While I was working on the first edition, a BBC producer, Denys Blakeway, was planning a BBC television documentary on the Windscale accident. He had contacted the AEA for assistance, and the Public Relations Office put him in touch with me. I worked with him on gathering the information he needed, though I did not appear in the excellent documentary, which was broadcast in 1990. He later became an independent television producer, and his production company, Blakeway Productions Limited, continues to produce high quality, award-winning documentaries on a wide range of topics. Denys and I have been friends since the original Windscale documentary, and I have had the pleasure of working with him on several other programmes.

Interest in the book was not confined to the UK. The explosion at Chernobyl in 1986 had stimulated public interest in the Windscale accident. In Vienna an international group of scientists, studying various aspects of the Chernobyl accident heard that my book was nearing completion. They were especially interested because the Chernobyl reactors were of an unusual type, somewhat akin to the Windscale ones, though a great deal larger. So a typescript of the book was sent out to Vienna to see if it contained any relevant scientific information which might assist their enquiries.

Some time later, the author Piers Paul Read wrote to the AEA. He had visited Chernobyl and was writing a book on it for the general reader. He wondered if they would read over the draft and advise on any errors. They asked if I would read it for them. It proved to be a big job – there were many suggestions for small revisions. I asked Ken Duncan, Chief Medical Officer of the AEA, if he would also read it, and as a result the three of us met for lunch at Ken's house near Oxford to go through the suggested changes. Piers Paul Read was interesting, clever and receptive, and we got a marvellous insight into his experiences at Chernobyl. This turned out to be a very interesting project, and produced an excellent book.

After the publication of my Windscale book in 1992, it was time to return to the third instalment of the big official history. I did so with increased misgivings. We had started work on it in 1975, nearly twenty years earlier, and much of that time had been taken up with my work on the books about nuclear testing in Australia and the Windscale accident, and on records management. I was more convinced than ever that the blockbuster plan was unworkable, and I was also concerned by the marked deterioration in Margaret Gowing's health. She was working desperately hard, but was finding it difficult to achieve much.

Margaret retired from her AEA work in 1993. Her two research assistants had already moved on to other more promising appointments. I thought that perhaps the AEA Council would now close down the Historian's Office, and that the third instalment would never be written. To my surprise, the Council decided that, though I was now in my mid-seventies, I should stay on, and asked me how best to use the research material we had already gathered.

I offered to write a book on the British H-bomb programme. There was very little information in the public domain, and I knew I could rely on the help and cooperation of the Ministry of Defence and the Aldermaston scientists. After that, I hoped to write a book on the British Civil Nuclear programme.

I started the H-bomb book with great trepidation, knowing that it would be very difficult to produce anything that was accessible to the intelligent general reader as well as acceptable to experienced scientists. Why was I, sole survivor of the AEA Historian's Office, taking on such a commitment instead of following my retirement plans and going to study in Italy? As I worked I was sometimes close to despair, particularly after hearing that a distinguished Oxford physics professor (formerly a senior scientist at Aldermaston) was of the opinion that no-one would ever be able to write the H-bomb history from the available documentation – and certainly no one as ill-equipped, in his opinion, as I was. Nevertheless, I realized that I must do my best because much vital evidence, especially the accounts of the scientists who had participated in the early work, would otherwise be lost forever.

At Aldermaston there was an enormous accumulation of documents. There were big and frustrating gaps, some of which occurred because much important work was never recorded by these scientists, who solved problems by action and discussion, then recorded only the answer, perhaps no more than a mathematical formula. A senior scientist in the Ministry of Defence, Victor Macklen, told me that, furthermore, scientific records had been destroyed to an extent that was harmful not only to history, but even to the current work of the scientists themselves. The reason for such wholesale destruction was a ruling by the security authorities that no secret papers should be kept unless they were clearly essential for future work. Their anxiety about atomic leaks was so great, especially after the Fuchs affair and because of the implications for the hard-won US-UK defence agreement of 1958, that they ordered this destruction.

Even if the records had all been intact and perfectly organized, the scientific content would still have been very difficult – vastly more difficult than for the A-bomb. I did not plan to include a great deal of this science in my book, but I wanted to grasp enough to be able to explain clearly and accurately what the reader needed to understand. Fortunately, I was able to consult several experienced scientists, expert in various fields. They were patient and generous with their help, and very encouraging. Slowly a picture began to emerge, and I started to compose, not the draft chapters yet, but 'think pieces' on different topics. It was like trying to put together a gigantic jigsaw, with half the pieces missing and no picture on the lid of the box. I was enthralled.

Privileged access is especially valuable for nuclear history because of the exceptionally high proportion of classified material in this field. Privileged access opens up a wealth of scientific records, and so changes the nature of the research material – as well as increasing its volume. The official historian is then better able to study the complex relationships between policy, strategy, science, and technology, and to understand more fully the reasons, choices, problems, and constraints involved. The hard realities behind the high-level decisions can be seen more clearly.

There is another advantage for the official historian who is fortunate enough to be in Richard Hewlett's words 'writing from the inside'.[1] Hewlett found that – while maintaining a robustly independent stance within the employer department or organization – the historian can gain much from day-to-day contacts and co-operative relations with other staff, particularly those with first-hand knowledge of the period, and activities, being studied. My experience has been similar.

First-hand witnesses can be invaluable in explaining technical matters, filling in gaps in the record, and enriching and enlivening the background. Witnesses will usually open up freely to an official historian even if they are understandably cautious in talking about such sensitive matters to other researchers.

By luck, I acquired a most unusual research assistant. Kate Pyne was a mature student in her forties, with years of experience as an aircraft engineer, who was working towards a degree in history. She joined me in 1993. She was a gifted researcher, worked with frenetic industry, and brought a technical cast of mind to the task. It was a productive, if sometimes exhausting, partnership for the two years of her contract, and I was delighted when Aldermaston agreed to create a new post and to appoint her as their in-house historian.

By the mid 1990s, the end of my many years as the Historian for the AEA was in sight. A new regime had taken over in the AEA, and all my old friends were gone, including Andrew Hills, the Board member who had overseen the history project. The new management did not seem very interested in history, especially of nuclear weapons, since the AEA no longer had responsibility for Aldermaston and weapons work. The original budget for the H-bomb book, always provisional, was nearly exhausted. I was now supervised by a middle-ranking manager whose interest did not extend beyond the costs and exactly how many words I had written in the previous month.

My view of the situation was quite different. First, I was determined to rescue all that I could from the sad ruin of the third instalment of the official history. Second, I could not bear to see the waste of years of arduous research in archives to which no other historians had, or might ever have, access. Third, I had a strong sense

---

[1] R. G. Hewlett, 'Writing from the Inside', in Frank B. Evans and Harold T. Pinkett (eds.), Research in the Administration of Public Policy (Washington, DC: Howard University Press, 1975), pp 7–16.

of commitment and obligation to the many people whose work I had tried to explain and honour. Finally, I felt that this whole story was far too important not to be studied and made known as fully and truthfully as possible. In the future, this story could never be understood from the documentation alone, so incomplete and so often impenetrable. I felt this was the last chance, and the responsibility had fallen on me. I could not abandon it.

In 1996, the new management at AEA decided I should retire, whether the book was finished or not. The matter of the broken book contract could be sorted out by the Contracts branch. My retirement was marked by an official lunch at Harwell, with speeches, flowers and presents. Afterwards, I packed all my personal notes into the back of my car and took them home to finish the task. I was eighty years old, but was not ready to give up. Whether contractually bound or not, whether paid or not, I was determined to complete the book. My friends in the Ministry of Defence understood what I was doing, and found a small pot of money to pay for my typing expenses. Otherwise, I was now on my own, living and working alone.

I proceeded to finish *Britain and the H-Bomb* at home. Then I took it through the exacting process of security clearance, for much of the content was highly sensitive, sent it to the publishers, dealt with the proofs, and saw it through to publication. The book was finally published in 2001, five years after I left the AEA.

The book was very well received. I had not expressed opinions or taken sides on a hugely controversial topic. I had simply tried to describe and explain the history, to help people to make better-informed judgements. I had tried to write for three kinds of reader: the educated general reader, the historian and the scientist. I know of some satisfied readers in the first category, and no historians or scientists have complained, so I am content that it was a job well done.

I was lucky to have completed *Britain and the H-Bomb* when I did. The next year, in 2002, I was registered as blind. I had struggled with failing eyesight during my work on the book, and things were complicated by unsuccessful eye surgery. This was a severe blow for me, as reading has always been a great joy in my life, and the loss of sight makes research and writing very difficult.

I struggled on as a writer. As the 50th anniversary of Windscale approached, the publisher asked for a third, revised and updated

*Lorna at the time of the publication of
'Britain and the H-Bomb' - 2001*

edition. It came out in 2007 and aroused a great deal of public interest. This interest included an excellent BBC documentary: *Windscale: Britain's Biggest Nuclear Disaster*, timed to coincide with the anniversary of the Windscale accident in October. It is strange to think how strong a leitmotif Windscale was through nearly 50 years of my life, from 1959, when I was recruited into the field of atomic energy and worked in the Health and Safety branch, through to 2007, with the anniversary of the accident.

The producers of the documentary were counting on me to provide a commentary, which they would include in the film. When they telephoned me to arrange a time, I had just returned home from a long stay in hospital and was very weak. I truly wanted to do my best for the programme, but warned them that they came at their own risk, as I might not be able to do much for them.

When they arrived, we began the usual process of question and answer in which the questions are later deleted. At the first question I felt a moment of desperation: I had no idea. And then I heard an unexpected answer – in my own voice. From that point all went well. We proceeded with almost five hours of filming. The next day I was very tired, but glad I had done my best.

The response to the broadcast was extremely positive. The BBC received many letters, and I personally had about two dozen letters and phone calls, mostly from scientists praising the quality of the information in the programme.

Though I officially retired from the AEA in 1996, it seems as though my work as a nuclear historian has never quite come to an end, and it has led me into many activities, given me many unexpected opportunities and some very good friendships.

Chapter 15

Widening Horizons

While I was working in the AEA Historian's Office I found myself becoming occasionally involved in the outside world of academics, journalists, and broadcasters. Though at first I had worked in an isolated way in the back-room with Margaret Gowing, through these outside activities my horizons gradually widened, my circle of acquaintances grew, and some lifelong friendships were formed. It started simply enough. From time to time the Historian's Office received enquiries from the few other historians working in the field, at home and abroad. If Margaret did not have time to work on the response, she would ask me to do so. Inevitably, if any follow-up was needed, I would then be called in to assist.

This is how I got to meet John Simpson in the early 1970s. He was, a professor of International Relations at Southampton University. We both felt that bringing together people who were actively working in the nuclear industry and people with a historical perspective could improve understanding and communications. An initial meeting of historians, scientists, and civil servants – groups who had not been much in contact with each other before – led to a regular series of study groups involving twenty to twenty-five people, two or three times a year. Initially the participants sat on opposite sides of the table, and were reticent about communicating with people who had such different perspectives from their own. Gradually, meaningful and useful discussions began to take place, and as the participants opened up, they found their ideas enriched by these exchanges. On one occasion, I remember, I took a PhD student to a meeting, 'to see how the real world joins up'. Afterwards he remarked 'it blew my mind'.

The Southampton study group proved very useful and productive. Later, John Simpson established the Mountbatten Centre for International Studies at Southampton. I was invited to participate, and found the exchange of ideas very exciting. The work continued until his retirement, while my friendship with John continues to this day.

In a similar way, I met Peter Hennessy at the time a lead writer for *The Times*, now a Professor of Contemporary History at Queen Mary, member of the House of Lords, and a well known author. We became friends, and with time he would send me graduate students to discuss various aspects of history and research. I was delighted when he invited me to attend his Inauguration Lecture as the Chair of Contemporary History.

I also met Brian Cathcart, who was a journalist for the *Independent*, when someone at the Ministry of Defence suggested that he contact me. He was doing research for his book, *Test of Greatness: Britain's Struggle for the Atom Bomb*, and I talked with him about his plans for his work. This bright and enthusiastic journalist was a pleasure to work with, and when he asked if we could keep in touch, I was delighted. Brian writes on many topics, but recently returned to nuclear history with his book *The Fly in the Cathedral*, an account of the work of the Cambridge scientists who split the atom in 1932.

In the early 1990s, I came to know Dr Andrew Brown, an oncologist who was working at the National Radiological Protection Board at Harwell. He had just accepted a post at a cancer clinic in Massachusetts, and before he left he rang me up. He had been reading a paper on Sir James Chadwick, had been very impressed by him, and was surprised that the only biographical source was a brief memoir in the Annals of the Royal Society. Chadwick's discovery of the neutron in 1932 had led directly to the discovery in 1938 of nuclear fission, and Chadwick eventually participated in the Manhattan Project. Andrew asked if I knew of a life of Chadwick, or of someone working on one, and when I said no, he declared that he was going to have to try to write one himself. Since he was not going to be attached to an academic institution in the US, he asked if I could assist him by reviewing drafts and so forth. I warned him that it would be very difficult, with the source material in the UK, but that I would be glad to help.

The resulting book, *The Neutron and the Bomb: A Biography of Sir James Chadwick,* was a great success when it was published in 1997. Andrew and I became fast friends, and ever since I have been eager to hear about his new works. At first, we exchanged marked up drafts; when my sight deteriorated, Andrew would read me drafts in many long trans-Atlantic telephone conversations, which demanded great concentration. He has just published his third book, about Joseph Rotblat, a Polish-born physicist who worked with Chadwick.

It was a pleasure to become friends with such intelligent and thoughtful writers, and we have continued to collaborate ever since. Andrew and I have co-authored a paper on nuclear deterrence, while Peter and Brian were kind enough to contribute forewords for the third edition of my Windscale book.

Sarah Manwaring-White, a noted producer of current affairs programmes on television, approached Margaret in the early 1970s with plans for a programme about radioactive pollution of the seas around northwest Britain. I became involved because of my experience in the areas of health and safety. After the broadcast, I made some positive comments about the programme, and she suggested we should keep in touch, which we did until her premature death in 2007. I remember many pleasant lunch meetings with her in a favourite small restaurant in Piccadilly.

After the publication of my Windscale book, the outside world opened up to an even greater extent. As I mentioned, I participated in the two BBC documentary programmes about Windscale, the first in 1990, the second in 2007, which were timed to coincide with the 50th anniversary of the accident. By the time of the second Windscale documentary, I had acquired considerable experience of radio and television programmes about nuclear history and safety. I had assisted in the creation of the content and checking its accuracy, as well as appearing as a commentator, or as they are more inelegantly known, a 'talking head'.

My first radio adventure, however, was quite by chance. Margaret Gowing was scheduled to give a short talk on a BBC programme. On the morning of the broadcast, Margaret called me from her home in Canterbury: she was unable to make it to the studio. She asked me to ring up the BBC and apologise on her behalf. As it was to be a live broadcast, the producer was in a difficulty, and asked if I would stand in. With some reluctance – not only was I unprepared and without experience of broadcasts, I was also nervous of what Margaret's reaction would be – I agreed, and took a taxi to the studio. It was a baptism of fire, but fortunately all went well.

In the late 1960s or early 1970s, some years after the Windscale accident, I was asked by Radio Oxford to do a brief talk about the ecological and political effects of the accident. Over time, I became quite accustomed to speaking on radio and television programmes.

In the late 1980s Margaret was due to give a lecture about the life and work of Lord Christopher Hinton at the Science Museum. She had, as usual, carefully prepared her paper, which she would normally read verbatim. At the last minute she was unable to attend and asked if I would contact the organisers to let them know and apologise for her. I ended up giving the lecture myself without preparation or notes, and just hoped that the audience would be sympathetic with me as a last-minute stand-in. It seemed to go well enough.

One BBC radio programme that I particularly enjoyed doing was an episode in the series *A Room with a View*. The producers of the series would send an expert guest commentator to a room where an event of some historical significance had occurred. The guest commentator would provide an evocative description of the room and the event, painting a picture for the listener. I was asked to visit Rudi Peierls' study at the University of Birmingham, where the Frisch–Peierls Memorandum had been written in 1940.

In this memorandum, the relatively young physics professor Rudi Peierls and his colleague Otto Frisch discussed the possibility of constructing an atomic bomb from uranium 235. Previous work on the design of an atomic bomb had assumed that many tons of uranium would be required, and that it might be necessary to deliver such a weapon by ship. Frisch and Peierls suggested that by using only one pound of the isotope uranium 235 it might be possible to build 'a radioactive super-bomb'. The British Government studied the memo, and eventually shared the idea with the American government; it became the basis for the design used in the Manhattan Project, to which Rudi was an important contributor. After the war, Rudi returned to his professorship at the University of Birmingham. He was also a consultant to Harwell, and I had known him for many years, so I was delighted to present this part of his story.

The BBC sent a car to drive me to the University of Birmingham, and I became more and more anxious as the driver was unable to find the address. When I was finally delivered, it turned out that we could not go into the actual study where the memo had been written, as it was being renovated. So the interviewer and I cheated, and were ushered into another, similar study. The interviewer asked me questions, and I described these two physicists conceiving of a new approach that would change the world forever. After we finished, the interviewer and I talked about this important moment for a little while, and I was so pleased when he confided in me, 'I wish we could sit here and talk all night.'

Some productions caused disappointment. A brilliant and very senior BBC producer contacted me: he was creating a six part series entitled *The Nuclear Age*. He also recruited Sir John Hill, former director and chairman of the AEA, and Walt Patterson, the nuclear physicist and energy activist. Together, the three of us formed a consulting group on the series. I felt that the series was well planned and structured, and both John and I contributed to the scripts. The producer managed to line up interviews with some first class scientists, many of whom were elderly, and he was able to capture the thoughts of many of these prominent scientists before they passed away. When the series was nearing completion, there was a reorganization within the BBC administration and, as a cost saving move, the new director-general stopped production. 'Too high-brow,' he said, 'too expensive.' I was very disappointed with the cancellation, as this had promised to be a high quality, well-informed production.

For some of these documentaries that I did over the years, I received modest honorariums, £50 or £75, though the programme *The Nuclear Age* provided me with a £1000 fee. Working on documentaries certainly was not a way to make a living; it was a way to share the knowledge that I had gathered since I joined the AEA back in the late 1950s. I really enjoyed working on these productions, and made many friends. I marvelled at the cooperative effort of the production teams, and the skill with which the producers and their teams would routinely take on and master new topics. Contributing to television and radio productions was a satisfying and invigorating undertaking.

Over many years I gradually became involved in various activities related to my work as a nuclear historian, some of which do not fit neatly into a chronological narrative. These extramural activities were rewarding both for the joy of participating in them, and the friendships that they led to.

Rudi Peierls was responsible for introducing me to two women in 1983, Scilla Elworthy and Rosie Houldsworth, with whom I went on to form lasting friendships. Scilla had recently set up the Oxford Research Group (ORG)[1] from her home in Woodstock, with the mission to find out who the people are who really make the decisions about nuclear weapons, and to develop effective dialogue between nuclear weapons decision-makers and their critics. I found myself sympathetic to ORG's concerns about nuclear proliferation, and liked their careful approach of publishing rigorously objective research on the one hand, while facilitating constructive, non-confrontational behind-the-scenes dialogue with decision-makers on the other. I was invited to join ORG's first board of advisers, and participated in a number of their conferences and seminars. Scilla was awarded the Niwano Peace Prize for this work in 2003, and has been nominated three times for the Nobel Peace Prize.

During the 1980s, Rudi was actively engaged in rallying support for a 'nuclear freeze' in Oxford and both Scilla and Rosie, and their colleague Tony Thomson, took part in the early discussion meetings he convened in the Physics Department. Sometimes, Rudi I would go into the centre of Oxford to collect signatures in our private capacity, not identifying ourselves by our association with the AEA or the University. Rudi was one of the most brilliant men I have ever known, and the gentlest and most modest of men. Occasionally we would encounter a person who would express strong but misinformed opinions about nuclear weapons; Rudi would invariably respond politely, gently correcting any misinformation, but never invoking his authority as an expert.

I was not always confined to the archives or even a BBC studio. As time went on, I found myself invited to interesting conferences at home and abroad, where I widened my horizons further and made new friendships. In 1993 I went to my first international conference in Nice,

---

[1] http//www.oxfordresearchgroup.org.uk/

Rudi Peierls and Lorna in a teleconference with Los Alamos

as part of the Nuclear History Programme. There I met three scholars who would become special friends of mine: the very young Beatrice (now Professor) Heuser, Professor David Holloway of Stanford, and Professor John Baylis of Aberystwyth.

It was an exciting experience for me. One of the speakers was a Russian nuclear scientist, Yuri Smirnov – surely the first ever to be allowed to take part in a conference of this kind. He gave a most interesting and candid account of the Soviet weapons programme, and offered to show a film which had been specially made at the major Russian weapons site to celebrate the eightieth birthday of the famous scientist Yuli Khariton. With a few other people, I went to see this film; the commentary was translated for us by David Holloway. The film consisted of archive footage as well as fresh material, and was fascinating to a nuclear historian. It showed some of the great personalities of the Soviet nuclear programme, including I. Kurchatov and Yuli Khariton talking together. There was also some dramatic footage of Soviet nuclear weapon tests at Chelyabinsk. I was enthralled.

Though the film had been privately made, I was later able to acquire a copy from Moscow; it was, I think, the only one in England. This was during the Gorbachev window of opportunity: I do not think it would have been so easy for Yuri Smirnov to come to such a conference a few years later.

While I was in Nice, I had a brief conversation that highlighted for me the role of luck in my life, and in the lives of others. Breakfast at the conference was served buffet style, and you found a place to sit wherever there was space. One morning I had my breakfast with a distinguished American scholar. Glancing around, he remarked that all the conference members present had in varying degrees been pretty successful, and no doubt were well pleased with themselves – deservedly so. But, he pointed out, they might not be aware of how lucky they were – how good fortune had helped them to succeed. He said that people should always be aware of their good fortune, and be thankful for it. I could not help but agree with him, thinking back to the various improbable events in my own life, that eventually led me to a career with the AEA, and eventually, to my own presence at the conference as a writer of nuclear history.

Marburg was the venue for the next conference in the Nuclear History Programme series. It is a delightful German town which has one of the oldest universities in the country and a most imposing castle built on a hilltop so precipitous that the mediaeval upper town is reached from the lower town by a huge elevator built into the rock. It is a picturesque place, with its steep cobbled streets and mediaeval buildings, and wonderful views across the countryside.

The conference was held in an enormous hall in the castle, where our voices echoed among the high stone arches, with the occasional tourist giving us a curious glance as they wandered by. My contribution was a short paper on work in progress on the British H-bomb programme, for which I abandoned my notes and for which, to my surprise, I received a standing ovation. Our free time was enjoyably spent exploring and having endless conversations with our colleagues in cafés and beer-cellars.

In 1999 I chanced to hear of another nuclear history conference, a joint American/Russian undertaking to be held in Vienna. I discovered that there had been a previous conference three years earlier, and came upon three of the papers, two Russian and one American, in a science journal. This next in the series was clearly an important event, and I could see from the agenda that it would be rather incomplete without a British contribution. Further investigation revealed that the conference organizers had sent a general invitation to London, but that this had not been followed up. I passed the information on to the universities most likely to be interested and asked the Ministry of Defence if they wanted to 'show the flag'. They agreed. There was only a week left to register and submit contributions, so my former research assistant Kate Pyne and I got to work immediately on our papers. I spoke on the health and safety aspects of the H-bomb programme, and radiation problems, while Kate's talk covered the first British bomb tests. Two British academics came for a day and added their contributions.

It was an unusual conference in that it was tightly planned, and required much hard work from the participants. The timetable each day was filled with twenty minute lectures on a huge variety of subjects. They dealt in formidable detail with every imaginable aspect of the original nuclear weapons programmes. The conference was attended by around fifty delegates from the US and a similar number of Russians as well as us few British, who, although so few in number, managed five papers between us. The atmosphere was cordial, and I can only recall one rather sharp exchange between a Russian and an American speaker. The Cold War seemed very far away.

One of the more surprising papers was given by Vladimir Barkovski, who had been an intelligence officer at the Soviet Embassy in London in the early days. He had been the channel to Moscow for a quantity of nuclear secrets. He gave a candid and most interesting talk on the role which he had played so brilliantly.

All this took place in a lovely old ballroom with wonderful chandeliers in a small Imperial palace outside Vienna. Somehow we managed to find a little spare time for interesting discussions, and I had memorable conversations with some English-speaking Russian colleagues.

At the conclusion of the conference there was a celebration dinner in a country restaurant among the vineyards. Small tables were set along the whitewashed walls of a converted wine cellar. Inevitably the East occupied one side and the West the other. Presently an Austrian accordion player appeared, complete with lederhosen and a Tyrolean hat. He started by playing some folk songs, and then invited requests. There were far more calls from the Russian side, and soon they began to sing lustily. Then a woman scientist ran out into the centre and began to dance. She was quickly joined by other Russian colleagues who held hands in rings and circled vigorously up and down in the open space between the tables. Amid all this excitement, as they passed our table, one group seized me and pulled me into the dance. I was swept off my feet and whirled around. It was so fast and furious it was almost like flying! That was a joyful evening! As we left the restaurant, David Holloway remarked, 'Now you see why the Russians are so indestructible. They have such spirit!'

Next morning, everyone said goodbye and went home, but Kate and I had a free day before our flight, so we were able to spend hours tramping around Vienna, seeing as much as we could on this, our first visit.

A brief but most enjoyable excursion was to Paris, where I had been invited to give a talk at the *Centre d'Etudes de l'Histoire Militaire* at the Chateau de Vincennes. It was a friendly and intimate audience and, as they all spoke or understood English, they wisely preferred me to use my own language. My book on the British H-bomb programme was finished but not yet published, and my audience was interested to know how the British experience compared with the French. The chairman was Dr Bertrand Goldschmidt, whom I greatly liked and admired. He was one of the most experienced of nuclear scientists, having begun his scientific career as an assistant to Marie Curie. I did not know him well, but I was proud and glad to be acquainted with him.

Attending these conferences, I was reminded of the unusual perspective that I had brought to my work. I had two great advantages over journalists and academic historians. The first was that I was 'embedded'. Rather than just visiting occasionally from the headquarters in London or some university, I had an office in Aldermaston, and later Harwell, working side-by-side with the scientists and engineers who had been involved in the work. I was always aware of the risk of 'group-think', but I need not have worried: they were such a varied lot, constantly arguing and talking about their work, with a lot of different of points of view. I did not just interview the leaders and decision-makers; I talked to those who had actually worked in the field, and who had vivid memories which if not captured would be lost forever.

My second advantage was that I knew how to interpret the official documents, and I understood how inadequate a picture such documents provide without looking at the working papers and talking to the people involved. For example, you read the minutes of a Cabinet discussion, and you may think you know how a decision was taken. You probably do not. Apart from all the controversial bits – the arguments and digressions – that were tidied out of the way by the Cabinet Secretary, many things that 'everybody knew and took for granted' would never appear in the record. I was able to draw on my experience of not just being 'embedded' in various parts of the AEA, but having been embedded in various Government departments. I remember a colleague reviewing, quite critically, an historian's account of a particular inter-governmental negotiation, saying that 'this wasn't the way things were done'. Then he remarked that I had had the advantage of actually taking part in negotiations between British and American officials, and seeing how things actually worked. He was right that it makes a difference.

Some of my observations were confirmed by my interactions with recent students. As a retired, but still very active historian, I was delighted when professors that I knew sent their graduate and postgraduate students to me to discuss their work. I saw how some of them suffered from their lack of background in the workings of government organizations. While many of the students had done good research, they would come to conclusions that did not take into consideration the context in which the events they were researching had happened. I would find myself saying, 'Your reasoning is sound, but that's not what happened'. It is the dilemma faced by many historians: an analysis based solely on official documents may not give the flavour of decision making, the now-forgotten burning issues of the time that strongly influenced an approach, and the personalities that, through conflict or temperament, might lead to an unanticipated outcome. I was reminded, too, of Bill Penney's advice about the danger of taking documents at face value. I enjoyed helping these students by providing background and context, and came to know a new generation of historians interested in nuclear topics

The last of my excursions was the longest and most adventurous. Shortly before the publication of my book on the British H-bomb was due, I was invited to go to Stanford University for a two-day colloquium organized by David Holloway. Soon the plans were expanded to include dates at the Los Alamos National Laboratory and Sandia Laboratory in New Mexico, and the University of California at Santa Barbara. I was delighted, but very anxious about the problems of so much travel, since by this time my sight was rapidly failing. My American hosts agreed to invite someone of my choice to accompany me. I immediately suggested Kate Pyne, who by this time was installed at Aldermaston as their in-house historian. This arrangement would make it all possible for me and would be a wonderful opportunity for her. It worked out most successfully. By the time the trip began, my book had appeared in the UK but was not yet available in the United States, so I took as many copies as I could carry as gifts for my hosts.

One of the challenges of the trip was to deliver all of my lectures without the benefit of notes. By then, I was too blind to read, though I was still able to appreciate the outlines of the New Mexico and California landscape. With Kate's help, I was able to prepare for the two big lectures at Los Alamos and Stanford, for which visual aids were supplied. When it came to the smaller informal talks, I never knew what would be required of me, so I simply spoke off the cuff. On reflection, I believe the Ministry of Defence was very trusting to allow me to give unscripted talks on such a sensitive subject as the British nuclear programme.

The trip got off to a bad start, as I became faint on the long flight from London to San Francisco, and spent the last hour in an oxygen mask, feeling very inadequate. Next day I had the morning to prepare for the Stanford colloquium, which was to begin after lunch. I was awestruck when I saw the list of those attending: not simply faculty and post-graduate students, but over twenty internationally known distinguished scientists had been invited.

Before the meeting opened, a message came from the legendary nonagenarian physicist Dr Edward Teller. He had intended to come to the conference, but was not feeling strong enough. He was on campus and wished to talk to the two guest speakers, German Goncharov and myself. So accompanied by David Holloway and a Russian history professor, we were duly conducted into the study where the great man sat, heavily slumped in his armchair. After brief greetings, he said, 'I am going to ask you questions'. He pointed at me. 'You first.' He paused. 'What is your opinion of cloning?'

I was surprised and much relieved not to be asked some terrifying theoretical physics problem, which would have exposed me as an ignoramus and impostor. I was not an expert on cloning, but decided I could cope. I said that if he meant human reproductive cloning, I was thoroughly opposed to it: all the poor little monsters that preceded Dolly the Sheep were a dire warning. Dr Teller said that medical research was advancing very rapidly and I was extremely reactionary. He thought that if the procedures were all properly planned and controlled the human prospect was most promising. My Russian colleague expressed cautious agreement.

'Why do I favour human cloning?' Dr Teller enquired rhetorically.

'Because you want more Edward Tellers,' I thought to myself, and quietly waited for his reply.

'Because I wish for a clone of myself,' he said, and went on to explain that he wanted to know whether a clone of himself would develop as an infant mathematician in the same way as he had done. Still, by his own account, his precocious attraction to mathematics had been due to his passion for certainty, which the mixed languages of his childhood home – German and Hungarian – singularly failed to provide. After a little more talk about the future of meteorology, a great interest of his, we were led from the presence and back to the conference room.

Kate and I then drove off down the lovely coast road, with mountains to the left and beaches to the right, to the Spanish-style houses and old monasteries of Santa Barbara, where I had been invited to the University. I did two lectures there, both small and intimate, and very pleasant.

Edward Teller

I also spoke at Los Alamos, the US weapons laboratory. I went into the big lecture hall, where a huge crowd was sitting on the benches, windowsills and stairs. Here I was memorably introduced as a woman who shared her name with a can-can dancer (apparently, he had found a story on the Internet of a can-can dancer named Lorna Arnold), and who had been also been rebuked by Dr Teller for her reactionary views on human cloning. Everyone roared with laughter and clapped and stamped. After this rousing introduction, my lecture went down a storm!

My brief time at Los Alamos was very busy, with lots of interesting conversations and meetings. I was exhilarated by New Mexico, with its vast empty landscape, its great outcrops of rock in cathedral-like formations, its mountains, and its thin, brilliant atmosphere. It was a most enjoyable visit.

One occasion that stays in my memory was at the home of a history professor – now a good friend – who invited several colleagues and post-graduate students to an evening's conversation at his house.

He asked me to talk about some of my wartime and post-war experiences. One of the guests was an elderly Yugoslav, long settled in America. I spoke of British agents I had known after their return from Yugoslavia, when the Allies replaced Mihailović with Tito, and mentioned the name of one Jasper Rootham.

'Ah, Jasper!' the guest exclaimed. 'How is he? I knew him as a guerrilla fighter in the mountains of Serbia. Where is he now?' I was able to tell him that after the war, Jasper had become quite a high official in the Bank of England, and had died only recently.

In the past several years, I have been travelling less, as age and diminishing health have slowed me somewhat. I have worked with Rosie Houldsworth, whom I first met through her work at ORG, serving as a speaker in her *TalkWorks* series[2]. These are short documentaries designed to promote international effort to reduce and ultimately eliminate global nuclear threats. Around the time of my 96th birthday, Rosie released a trilogy of short films through the ORG website, in which I talk about current nuclear issues. I have written articles with the historian Andrew Brown on nuclear deterrence that have appeared in journals such as *International Relations*. I have also worked on this memoir, which has allowed me to look back on a long life with many surprising events.

One pleasant aspect of longevity is that you may find yourself receiving honours. I have become a Fellow of the Institute of Physics, a rare thing for a non-scientist, and have an Honorary Fellowship in the Society for Radiological Protection. In 2009, I was awarded an Honorary Doctorate of Letters by the University of Reading, where Professor Beatrice Heuser delivered a kind speech summarizing my career. Though I was unable to attend the ceremony due to ill health, I wish that I could have done so, because of the many friends, family and colleagues who came to the ceremony. I never could have anticipated when I left Bedford College in 1937 with a BA in English, that I would some day be so honoured for my work in nuclear history.

---

[2] See http://www.talkworks.info for these films, and others on nuclear topics.

Chapter 16

On Reflection

When I reflect upon my life, one of the greatest sources of joy has been the lasting friendships, many of which arose through my work, and which have developed into a widening network. I have already spoken of many of these friends in earlier chapters, but I would like to mention a few who did not fit neatly into the narrative.

I met Dennis Hay when I was working at the War Office. Like Margaret Gowing, he was involved in the project to write an official history of World War II. After the War, he became a lecturer, and eventually a Professor of Medieval and Renaissance History at the University of Edinburgh. His researches led him and his wife Gwyneth to visit Italy for extended periods, and they would often invite me to stay with them. I visited their flat in the centre of Rome when Dennis was doing research in the Papal Library. Another time, Dennis was working at the University of Florence, and they rented a lovely villa just outside the city. My visits with them led to my happy love affair with Italy.

The Hays also introduced me to another dear friend, the historian Geoffrey Best. We first met when he was a lecturer at the University of Edinburgh, but our friendship only really began many years later when he retired to Oxford. I see him and his wife Marigold frequently, and he sometimes reads books or articles to me. He has widened my historical interests, while I have introduced him to scientific and especially nuclear history.

In 1959, I shared an office at the AEA with Ken Binning, an enthusiastic young man fresh from the Treasury. Ken was later transferred to Risley, in the north of England, and he and his wife Pam moved up to Manchester. Our families became close friends: my boys spent holidays with the Binnings, and my son Geoff remembers

Ken and Pam Binning

pushing the youngest Binning in her pram. Geoff also worked with Ken at the Programmes Analysis Unit at Harwell in 1968. Ken went on to become the Director General of the Anglo-French Concorde supersonic airliner project, after which he and Pam retired to southeast London. The three of us, and our extended families, remained close friends until Ken and Pam's recent deaths.

Through the Binnings, I met the writer Madeline Riley. I made her acquaintance at one of the Binnings' lunch parties, and she surprised me by following up with a letter suggesting that we might meet for lunch. I agreed, and for many years we met regularly at a favourite Italian restaurant in Oxford. Now that I can no longer rendezvous in the city, Madeline comes to my home for a quiet lunch and a lively conversation whenever she is in Oxford.

It was at a meeting hosted by John Simpson of the Mountbatten Centre for International Studies that I first met Christopher Watson, now Chair of the British Pugwash Group. A theoretical physicist, he had worked at the AEA, but I had not known him then. He and his wife Anne, who is a doctor, are an energetic couple with a wide variety of interests. They visit me frequently, and we have a shared interest in Pugwash activities.

Although I am now practically housebound, I am never lonely, and take great pleasure in the frequent and engaging visits and phone calls from friends old and new. Oxford has proved a convenient and central location to live. Some of my professorial colleagues have enriched my life by sending me graduate students, with whom I discuss their work. It is good to see a new generation of historians and political scientists interested in the issues of nuclear weapons and deterrence. I am still in touch with my many academic and journalist friends, and appear from time to time in television and radio programmes. Besides the social connection, I greatly value the continued involvement in my familiar world of work. I do not yet feel quite retired.

My siblings and extended family visit me frequently, and my son Stephen lives and works in Oxford. My older son Geoffrey lives in California, but is always a welcome visitor.

As I reflect back over my more than ninety-five years of life, my short century, what are some of the significant changes that I see? Certainly the role of women in our society has changed dramatically. My parents were children of the nineteenth century, and many of the voices in my earliest years were undeniably Victorian. My grandmother constantly told me to 'be good, sweet maid, and let who will be clever', because being clever was not the mark of a nicely brought-up little girl. Any signs of cleverness resulted in Granny warning me that I would have to sit on the 'Stool of Repentance', or be sent to the 'House of Correction'. These early teachings discouraged me in some ways, and made me feel that I must be in someway not good enough.

I often found myself a woman in a man's world, during and just after the War, and later in the AEA. Back then, it was high praise to be told that I was 'just like one of the chaps.' Today it is assumed that women are capable, and can choose their own path, not always dependent on the whims of the men and authorities in their lives. My generation grew up in a gap in the political efforts for women's rights, after the crusading suffragettes, and before the women's movement of the 1970s. Nevertheless, our lives changed substantially because of the two world wars, and the economic and technological changes that took place. These included, in the domestic sphere, the introduction of time savers such as convenience foods and supermarkets, and labour saving devices such as washing machines and refrigerators. In the personal sphere, the new availability in the 1960s of the contraceptive pill gave the generations that came after us control over when they have children. These technological changes enabled women to take greater advantage of opportunities to seek varied employment outside the home.

I remember a childhood that was in many ways idyllic, despite the hard work and poverty of our farm life. I vividly remember the rural landscapes, filled with the wild flowers that were so much a part of our everyday existence, and so many of which have almost disappeared. Though our modern existence brings us many advantages, there is an appeal to that quieter time. Even now, on a restless night, I sometimes lull myself to sleep by playing a game of listing the wild flowers of my youth. I find much comfort in the memory of that greener, more rural English countryside.

In reflecting on my career, it can only be characterised as 'unexpected'. Over seventy years ago, I beat an inglorious retreat from the teaching profession, leaving Derbyshire with no idea of what I would do next. The intervention of the War relieved me of any decision about next steps; I was recruited into His Majesty's Service, and for the next eight years I served my country to the best of my ability.

Those years were fascinating, filled with interesting people and experiences, and I learned many skills that I was to find useful. But they were equally filled with difficult experiences, living with the daily danger and uncertainty of the War, and the horrific conditions in occupied Berlin. I am proud to see how successful the Control Commission for Germany was in its efforts to assist the restoration of Germany after the War, so unlike the disastrous peace settlement after the First World War. The successful creation of a democratic, peaceful and prosperous post-war Germany was due at least in part to Allied policies in which Britain played a leading role, not always remembered today.

After having two sons, I found myself in the rather unusual situation of a being a single parent, and had to find work again, taking whatever jobs I could find to pay the bills and put food on the table. I had no career, merely a string of temporary jobs.

Lorna and her sister Ruth Smith, 2011

Then, Fortune took a hand, in the guise of a chance lunchtime encounter with a former colleague. I joined the UKAEA, even though I felt completely unsuitable. I had no science credentials, and no knowledge of this kind of work. Nevertheless, I was absorbed into the brave new world of science and technology, and found that I had reached my destination - a career which was to occupy me for the next forty years. To my surprise, I found that much of my previous experience had prepared me well for my work in the Health and Safety Branch of the AEA. And I felt that after many years of wandering, I had found work that meant a great deal to me. It provided comradeship and a feeling of satisfaction as we worked together. It also gave us a sense of purpose as we tried to establish policies and guidance on how to work safely with radiation.

Then in 1967, I was asked to take on yet another role within the AEA, working as a nuclear historian, a role in which I had little interest. My first work as historian, with Margaret Gowing, was in the tradition of the British Official War Histories, a detailed account of British nuclear history from 1945-1952, delivered in two hefty volumes.

Eventually, I developed my own style, which tried to address a wide audience: intelligent lay-people, scientists, historians, and policymakers. The books that I wrote were less the work of a leisured historian than a response to relatively immediate needs. In the case of Windscale, we had to move quickly because of the impending release of Government documents. The book on the Australian tests was provoked by the actions of the Australian Commission, and the need to provide accurate information to counterbalance the sensationalist reporting. We had always planned to cover the topic of British H-bomb programme in the next volume of the comprehensive Official History. When that project foundered, it was important to ensure that the research and preparatory work would not be lost, and with the support of the Ministry of Defence I was able to do so.

In my books I tried to be accurate and objective, and to allow the reader to draw conclusions. Suppressing my personal opinions was not without risk: some of my friends and family imagined that my association and even friendships with those who produced nuclear weapons meant that I fully endorsed the development of those weapons. I was also aware that as an official historian I was open to the suspicion of being a 'company spokeswoman'. I inevitably thought a great deal about nuclear weapons and was delighted to be asked by Rudi Peierls to assist in 'Freeze' movement in the 1980s. I have been engaged in similar activities ever since, and I am very much opposed to nuclear weapons, as well as civil nuclear power.

Even though I was a reluctant recruit into the Historian's Office, and in spite of the repugnance I feel about nuclear weapons, I am glad that I became a nuclear historian. I have had access to the full records, including the most restricted material, and I have been able to talk directly to the scientists, engineers, and officials involved. This has given me a unique opportunity to provide a detailed and thorough historical account of some of the key events in British nuclear history. Writing nuclear history is hard work because one needs to consider so many aspects – political, economic, strategic, social, as well as scientific – but without exploring all of these factors, it is impossible to fully understand the decisions of those involved.

Nuclear power, both military and civil, has been and continues to be highly controversial. Much of what has been written is polemical, and some is scientifically inaccurate, and it is difficult to obtain a truthful and comprehensive picture of either civil or military programmes. In these circumstances, I feel that those who are in a position to provide accurate and unbiased information have a moral obligation to do so.

When I left the farms of my childhood and went to university, it seemed that my future was assured, that I was so lucky. I discovered that Fortune could be fickle. Fortune took me in many directions, some gratifying, some difficult. Then I found a career with the AEA that became my life's work, work of which I was proud, and which had great meaning, and I hope, value to others. It gave me the opportunity to work with intelligent and fascinating people, and I made many good friends who have enriched my life. On reflection, in my short century, Fortune has been far more my friend than my foe.

Publications

A partial list of publications by Lorna Arnold

Books

Arnold, Lorna (1987) A Very Special Relationship: British Atomic Weapon Trials in Australia. London: HMSO Books. ISBN 0-11-772412-2.

Arnold, Lorna & Pyne, Katherine (2001) Britain and the H-Bomb London: Palgrave Macmillian ISBN 0-312-23518-6

Arnold, Lorna & Smith, Mark (2006) Britain, Australia and the Bomb: The Nuclear Tests and Their Aftermath (International Papers in Political Economy) London: Palgrave Macmillian ISBN 1-4039-2101-6

Arnold Lorna (2007) Windscale 1957: Anatomy of a Nuclear Accident London: Palgrave Macmillian ISBN 0-230-57317-7

Gowing, Margaret & Arnold, Lorna (1974) Independence and Deterrence: Britain and Atomic Energy, 1945-52: Volume 1: Policy Making
London: Macmillan. ISBN 0-333-15781-8

Gowing, Margaret & Arnold, Lorna (1974) Independence and Deterrence: Britain and Atomic Energy, 1945-52: Volume 2: Policy Execution.
London: Macmillan. ISBN 0-333-16695-7

Articles

Arnold, Lorna (2000) A Letter from Oxford: The History of Nuclear History in Britain, Minerva 38: 201–219, 2000.

Brown, Andrew & Arnold, Lorna (2010) The Quirks of Nuclear Deterrence, International Relations Vol 24(3): 293–312

Picture Credits

FAMILY PHOTOS

Family photos were provided by Lorna Arnold and members of the Arnold and Rainbow families. Special thanks to Ruth Smith for her contributions.

OTHER PHOTO SOURCES

Airship Heritage Trust

Coastal Class Airship
http://www.airshipsonline.com

Normandy Historians & P. Blakiston

Wanborough School
http://www.normandyhistorians.co.uk

NDA Photo Library, UK Atomic Energy

Lorna Arnold in the 1970s
Lorna Arnold in the 1990s
Margaret Gowing
Christopher Hinton
Dr Andrew McLean
Bill Penney

Rosie Houldsworth

Lorna Arnold and Ruth Smith

Royal Holloway College, University of London, Archives

Lorna Rainbow at Bedford College

Wikimedia Commons

Allied Control Council Building
http://en.wikipedia.org/wiki/File:Berlin_kammergericht.jpg
Berlin, 1945
http://upload.wikimedia.org/wikipedia/commons/f/f9/
Bundesarchiv_B_145_BildP054320%2C_Berlin%2C_Brandenburger_Tor
_und_Pariser_Platz.jpg
Edward Teller
http://commons.wikimedia.org/wiki/File:Edward_Teller_(later_years).jp
g
Map of Zones of Germany
http://upload.wikimedia.org/wikipedia/commons/b/b3/Allied_Occupat
ion_Zones.jpg

Index

A

Lightning Source UK Ltd.
Milton Keynes UK
UKOW02f1912250416

272958UK00001B/127/P